SUMMITS AND TRAILS

SUMMITS AND TRAILS

By

Gary Yates

E-BookTime, LLC
Montgomery, Alabama

Summits and Trails

Copyright © 2005 by Gary Yates

All rights reserved. No part of this book may be reproduced or transmitted in any form or by any means, electronic or mechanical, including photocopying, recording, or by any information storage and retrieval system, without permission in writing from the copyright owner.

Library of Congress Control Number: 2005937835

ISBN: 1-59824-099-4

First Edition
Published December 2005
E-BookTime, LLC
6598 Pumpkin Road
Montgomery, AL 36108
www.e-booktime.com

CONTENTS

Introduction 7
Part One - Summits 9
Part Two - Trails 119

Introduction

The climbing journal is an account of two decades of mountain climbing. I started keeping a record of my climbs at the very beginning of my introduction to mountaineering, a pursuit that has given me and my wife, Karla, many great experiences, and one that has led us to the summits of mountains in the United States, Canada, Mexico and Scotland. Many of the journal entries are brief, but they bring back great memories of wonderful days on the mountains.

Soon after we became interested in mountain climbing, Karla and I joined the Glacier Mountaineering Society (GMS). This is a group made up of people with like interests, including a great love for Glacier National Park in Montana. Some of the members met their spouses while working at the park when they were of college age. Today, those same folks are bringing their children and grand children back to Glacier National Park for a few days each summer to attend the annual reunion of the GMS and to do some hiking and climbing, and to meet once more with old friends.

Many of the climbs recorded in the following pages took place in Glacier National Park. Most of these were done with members of the Glacier Mountaineering Society. Denis and Shi Twohig, founders of the mountaineering society, were on many of these climbs, sometimes as climb leaders, other times as enthusiastic members of the climbing groups.

As our climbing experience and skills increased, we began climbing outside the boundaries of the park. The Grand Teton, Mt. Rainier, Mt. Whitney, Mt. Adams and Pico de Orizaba are just a few of the summits outside the park that we and other GMS members have reached.

The journal accounts of our climbs of Popocatepetl, Iztaccihuatl and El Pico de Orizaba is combined. I chose to elaborate on these mountains because of their high altitude, and because Orizaba is the third highest mountain in North America.

The brief length of the entries for some of the mountains we climbed in no way lessens the experiences that we had on them. Each and every one of them were very special in their own way.

Following the mountain climbing section are journal entries from a few of the many other interesting experiences that Karla and I have shared. These entries tell about adventures such as hiking on the Pacific Coast, exploring Aravaipa Canyon, and sea kayaking on the Johnstone Strait, out from Port Hardy, BC.

Trekking in Nepal was a special experience. In keeping a journal of our trip, I found that the spelling of names of villages and places can vary a bit, depending on the local maps, books, or signs that one uses as a source of information. I used the spelling that appeared to be appropriate.

All photos in this book were taken by the author.

PART ONE

CLIMBING JOURNAL

* * * * * * *

* * * * *

Colors of the Past

*The colors of the days gone by,
like paintings flying in the wind,
drift across the star filled sky.*

*Where moon and silver clouds begin
to dash along their windswept flight
above the lofty peaks so high.*

*Like prisms hanging in the sun
on webs of silk, they fly on by.*

* * * * *

Gary Yates

Climbing in Glacier National Park

"Rock!" The call rings out sharply through the crisp mountain air. Everyone in the party instantly looks upward, ready to take evasive action. A football size missile careens wildly down the couloir, the sound of its fall echoing through the cliffs around us. Tensed muscles relax as silence returns once more to the peak.

These young mountains are noted for their loose and crumbling rock, and their ledges are covered with debris of varying sizes, giving the effect in some instances of standing on ball bearings. A mere sixty million years old, their summits are sharp, and their ridges raw and knifelike. Here a climbing helmet is a necessity one cannot afford to be without.

Our small group was nearing the top of the class 4 and 5 couloir on the great east face of Mt. Clements, one of several prominent peaks surrounding the Logan Pass area of Glacier National Park. Each of us had experience climbing in the park, and were very much aware of the hazards of rock fall. In this narrow and steep couloir we felt particularly vulnerable, and for safety we climbed the more dangerous pitches one at a time.

Huddling behind a projecting ledge while awaiting my turn, I looked down to the base of the cliffs and the glacial

Summits and Trails

moraine almost 2,000 feet below. From that gray talus mound, wildflower covered slopes reached gently downward towards the Going-to-the-Sun road, which winds its way across the continental divide at Logan Pass. The visitor center parking lot appeared the size of a postage stamp. The road was visible for several miles, winding its way down to the deep blue of St. Mary's Lake to the east, which lay shimmering beneath the towering red cliffs of Red Eagle Mountain. To the west I looked down onto the top of Mt. Oberlin, while across the valley loomed the 9,000 foot summit ridge of Mt. Pollack.

One by one we made our way up the couloir, topping out just a few yards from the summit cairn. The view was fantastic. In every direction peaks of mountains jutted through swirling clouds in an array of gray and silver pinnacles.

After adding our names to the summit register, and enjoying a quick lunch, we started working our way down by an easier route, following a goat trail high up on the north face, and coming out on a grassy saddle far above Hidden Lake. We were in high spirits as we headed back along the trail which wound its way through bear grass and sub-alpine fir. What a wonderful climb it had been! How lucky we were to have such easy access to some of the most spectacular mountains in the northwest!

A few of these mountains had been climbed by adventuresome white men several years before Glacier became a national park in 1910. George Bird Grinnell, Henry Stimson and James Willard Schultz were some of those early adventurers. Schultz and Grinnell played major roles in park history, and gave Indian names to many of the peaks.

Four years after the park was established, the Seattle Mountaineers, 115 members strong, did some extensive climbing here. In the early twenties the well known mountaineer Norman Clyde made many first ascents. In the following years the park continued to see more climbers on its peaks, with local mountaineers as well as climbing clubs from around the country making it a summer meeting place. During the 1960's climbing became very active, and the popularity continues today. But still the high country remains relatively uncrowded.

Most rock climbers avoid these mountains, preferring instead the more solid pitches of limestone and granite found in other ranges, where handholds are more secure, and difficult routes accept pitons, chocks and nuts more readily. Alpine climbers, however, find these peaks to be a never ending source of pleasure, beauty and excitement.

The majority of these mountains, like mountains everywhere, offer a variety of routes to the top, with varying degrees of difficulty. Many can be climbed by scrambling, while some require only an occasional belay. Others, like Mt. Wilbur near Many Glacier on the eastern slope of the divide, challenge the more experienced climbers. Mt. St. Nicholas, considered to be the most difficult in the park for climbers, offers no "easy" way up. The last thousand feet of vertical on this pyramidal peak consists of class 4 and 5 pitches, with several rappels required on the descent.

The rewards at the summits are great. Climbers see a world that the average park visitor cannot imagine exists. Surrounded by seemingly limitless vistas of snow capped peaks, sparkling turquoise lakes set in hanging valleys, and cirques containing remnants of great glaciers that helped form this magnificent area, mountaineers become addicted to these routes, and many return year after year to climb the great peaks.

One distinct advantage to climbing in Glacier Park is the accessability of its mountains. Many can be climbed in a day if one gets a reasonably early start. And there are

Summits and Trails

plenty of peaks available, more than enough to keep the average climber busy for years, if he or she is inclined to try and reach the summits of as many as possible.

While many of Glacier's mountains are in the 8,000 and 9,000 foot range, with actual climbing elevation gains ranging from 3,000 to 5,000 feet, there are six peaks in the park that exceed 10,000 feet. Some of these are more remote than others. Mt. Cleveland, the highest at 10,466 feet, can best be reached by taking a boat from Waterton Townsite in Canada's Waterton Park, and base camping from there.

Mt. Merritt, reaching an altitude of just over 10,000 feet, can be approached by a beautiful trek through Glacier's Belly River country. This journey is an experience in itself. The trail from the Chief Mountain Customs Station passes through miles of beautiful meadows and forests, before crossing a stream on a suspension bridge and continuing beside sparkling waterfalls and lakes.

This area of the park is one of the most scenic that Glacier has to offer, and Mt. Merritt affords the most spectacular views to be found anywhere. On its summit immediately above Old Man Glacier, which flows eastward from just below the summit cairn, one is greeted by a breathtaking panorama of high lakes nestled in ice-bound cirques, beneath peaks extending into Canada and reaching far to the northern and western horizon. Several valley lakes are visible far below, and neighboring major peaks reach towards the heavens.

While rock fall is the primary objective hazard to be encountered while climbing in the park during the summer season, there can be occasional lightning. Although the area is not subject to the severe electrical storms found in other parts of the Rocky Mountains, some of the peaks seem to be more susceptible than others. The 9,642 foot high Going-to-the-Sun Mountain is one of these. While at the summit cairn last summer, I discovered that the one foot long piece of thick walled plastic pipe that held the summit register had been struck by lightning, burning a hole in each end and charring the notebook inside!

    Avalanche potential makes winter climbing conditions generally extremely hazardous, and while climbing is permitted during the winter months, rangers tend to discourage it. Only those with a lot of experience with snow and ice should attempt winter climbs in the park.

    On the eastern slope of the divide, rising majestically at the edge of the sprawling prairie, stands Chief Mountain, a 9,080 foot high mountain of unusual formation, and a prominent landmark in the area. Its east face appears formidable and intimidating, but there are routes up it. It is most easily climbed from the west, however, with that route being for the most part a scramble. Its lofty summit has been used by Indians as a place of vision quest for no one knows how many centuries, and is still a place of spiritual significance for the Blackfeet, whose reservation borders the mountain. It remains the site of Indian ceremonies, and climbers should enter the area with that in mind. On its narrow summit one can see the obvious places where men must have spent many hours, or even days, waiting for the spirits to grant them a vision that would guide their lives.

    A lifelong sport, and enough mountains to last a lifetime. What a combination to be found here in Montana's crown jewels of the nation!

Summits and Trails

A typical mountain scene in Glacier National Park. A sea of beautiful, rugged peaks await the adventurous climber.

Climbing Journal

Chief Mountain 9,080 ft.

North Central area, Glacier National Park.

Summer, 1984.

Chief Mountain is a striking landmark. Located near the eastern edge of Glacier National Park, it has played, and continues to play a significant role in Blackfeet Indian culture. We saw medicine bundles in the trees along the trail at the foot of the mountain.

There were 5 of us in our group; Karla, George, Kate, Becky and myself. We ascended the west talus route. At each step in the loose talus, one's foot would slip backward a few inches. The talus made it tough going on the ascent, but it also gave a quick and fun descent on our way down from the summit.

Mostly class 2 and 3, with one short class 4 pitch near the summit. Elevation gain 3,800 feet.

This was the first mountain that Karla and I had ever climbed. We are looking forward to climbing many more.

Summits and Trails

Great Northern Mt.   8,720 ft.

Great Bear Wilderness, Montana.

In June of 1986, six of us ascended the class 2 and 3 western ridge approach in good weather. We camped overnight at 6,900 feet in the saddle on the ridge. The Stanton glacier reaches the summit ridge on the east side. A trail traverses the west slope before reaching the summit. Nice views of the surrounding wilderness from the summit. Elevation gain 4,471 feet.

We descended the same route we had gone up. Rain was starting to fall when we reached our vehicles.

Divide Mountain   8,650 ft.

St. Mary Valley, Glacier National Park

June 29, 1986. It took our group of seven climbers about 2 hours to climb the class 2 and 3 route up past the old fire lookout to the summit of Divide Mountain, and 1 ½ hours to come back down. Much of the approach for this route is on the Blackfeet Indian Reservation.

It was raining lightly when we left our vehicles at the trailhead, but we continued on with our climb anyway, hoping that the skies might clear. The weather was cloudy and stormy all the way up and back, but the clouds were high enough that we had good visibility, so the view from the summit was good.

Mt. Aeneas   7,530 ft.

Jewel Basin, Montana.

In July of 1986, after driving to the trail head high in the mountains east of the Flathead Valley, four of us followed the class 2 route along Aeneas ridge to the summit. It was a gradual, easy climb, with a trail most of the way.

Weather was beautiful, and visibility was great. The wilderness area and views of the surrounding mountains made the climb very worthwhile. I had climbed Aeneas by the same route the previous April. The route was snow covered then, and I used X-country skis much of the way.

Mt. Gould   9,553 ft.

Garden Wall and Logan Pass area, Glacier National Park.

July 21, 1986. Our group of twelve climbers started at the Weeping Wall area along the Going-to-the-Sun Road and ascended the class 3 route to the summit via the Gem Glacier route. Elevation gain 3,600 feet. There is a short coulier on the route up to the summit from the Gem notch where we experienced some interesting climbing, but no belay was requested by any of the party.

There were wonderful views in every direction from the summit, which we all enjoyed while Ed found a rock to sit on near the summit cairn and played a melody on his flute.

Summits and Trails

A climber works her way up Divide Mountain. In the valley below, St. Mary Lake lies serene and still on a cloudy day in Glacier Park.

Viewed from the summit of Mt. Oberlin, Mt. Gould dominates the horizon. Gem Glacier lies hidden just through the notch in the left of

In the spring, snow still remains on the mountains near Logan Pass in Glacier Park.

There was quite a lot of loose rock on this mountain, especially on our descent down the face above the Big Bend and Weeping Wall area. This was a more direct route back to the Going-to-the-Sun Road at the Big Bend then the one we had taken on our ascent. Great weather.

Mt. Reynolds 9,125 ft.

Logan Pass area of Glacier National Park.

August, 1986. From the Logan Pass parking lot on a beautiful day, Karla and I hiked the 10 mile round trip to the summit of Mt Reynolds in about 6 hours. The wild flowers were beautiful all along our approach to the base of the mountain. We tried to avoid stepping on them as we hiked along.

We took the south-west talus slope route to the summit, a class 2 and 3 climb with an elevation gain of 2,500 feet.

From the summit there were grand views of Hidden Lake and Dragon's Tail, and for miles in every direction. The parking lot looks postage stamp size when viewed from the top of Reynolds and other surrounding peaks.

Warrior 7,905 ft.   **Gildart Peak** 7,903 ft.

Swan Range east of the Flathead Valley, Montana.

On August 30, 1986, Karla, Ron, Diane and myself were on

a backpacking trip along the southern end of Alpine Trail number 7. This was a great scenic hike, and we scrambled up these two small peaks that were just a short distance off the trail.

Easy climbing with little elevation gain, but the summits afforded a view of the surrounding area that we could not get from the trail.

This was our second attempt to reach Gildart Peak and Lake. Our first trip was memorable for the steady downpour of rain, which kept up for hours. We also missed a turnoff for the trail to Gildart and ended up setting up our tents for the night in a clearing beside a game trail that led down the west slope of the mountains, and away from our intended destination.

The weather was fine on this trip, no rain storms like we had the last time.

Mt. Vaught   8,850 ft.

Glacier National Park, McDonald Creek area.

September 1986. Denis, Shi and me. Our ascent route was up Howe ridge to the summit of Mt. Stanton, then we followed the ridge between Stanton and Vaught to the summit of Mt. Vaught.

The elevation gain was 5,650 feet. Class 2 and 3, with a few class 4 pitches on a 50 foot traverse of the ridge between Stanton and Vaught. A rope belay was used at one short pitch.

Beautiful weather. A fantastic ridge route with spectacular views. Only a half dozen climbers had signed the summit register since 1970. We left a new register on the summit. This climb was a 12 hour round trip from the Trout Lake trail head.

Mt. Oberlin 8,180 ft.

Glacier National Park, Logan Pass area.

October 26, 1986. Karla and I started from the Logan Pass parking area, then hiked across beautiful flower covered meadows to the scree slope below the summit. This late in the year the park does not have the number of visitors that are there during the summer, and there were very few people at the pass. We were the only ones on the summit.

With an elevation gain of about 1,500 feet, it was an easy class 2, short, fun climb, and we had a nice view down into the McDonald Creek valley and also over towards the Livingston Range.

Mt. Henry 8,847 ft.   **Mt. Appistoki** 8164 ft.

Two Medicine area of Glacier National Park.

June 6, 1987. Cool, sunny, windy day, great climbing

weather. Denis, Shi, Mike, Tom, Jennifer, Vic, Brenda, Karla and I ascended the Scenic Point route to the summit of Mt. Henry, and then went on to the summit of Appistoki. Our descent route was the upper east side of Appistoki. Total distance about 13 miles. Class 3 with a bit of class 4 at the summit of Mt. Henry. The round trip took 11 hours, 2 of which were spent finding a route off of Appistoki.

After checking out the cliffs at the north end and the west side, we found the best way down to be about 500 feet north of the summit. We dropped down the east side of Appistoki to the stream bed.

Red Mountain   9,400 ft.

Two Medicine area, Glacier National Park.

June 14, 1987. A little over 9 hours round trip, class 3 with some class 4. Elevation gain 5,000 feet. Denis, Shi, Karla and I, Brenda, Dale, Jan, Dan, Ev and Sarah did the climb in perfect weather.

Our ascent route was via the Dry Fork, then the Ptarmigan Trail for 1 hour, then up the south slope to the ridge. This mountain apparently has not been climbed often, as only a few climbers had signed the register. It was last signed in 1971 by Jerry DeSanto, and no one had signed it in the past 5 years.

Painted Tepee   7,650 ft.

Two Medicine area of Glacier National Park.

June 28, 1987. On a cool and cloudy day, our group which included Denis, Shi, Karla, Dale, Co, Betsy, and Rebecca did the round trip to the summit and back in 9 hours. Our approach was by way of the Two Medicine Pass trail. The route was mostly trail, class 2 with a bit of class 4 at the small summit peak. There was loose rock at the narrow summit. Elevation gain about 2,500 feet. It was about a 21 mile round trip.

On the way back, not far from Two Medicine, the trail was a boardwalk for a short distance. When Karla and I walked onto the boardwalk, a family of Pine Martin scurried from underneath it and disappeared in the tall grass and underbrush. It was a treat to see them at such close range.

The long hike was worth it, as the view from the summit was unique, and the unexpected encounter with the family of Pine Martin provided an unusual and memorable experience. They were in no great hurry to get away, and it was fun for us to be able to observe the mother trying to keep track of her young ones as they wandered off into the undergrowth along the trail.

Carthew Peak   8,550 ft.   **Mt. Buchanan**   8,500 ft.

Waterton Park, Canada.

July 4, 1987. Our group included Denis, Shi, Karla, Dale

and Chester. We shuttled to Cameron Lake, and then took the trail to Carthew Ridge. Very nice weather, and we had an easy walk to Carthew Peak. From there we proceeded along the ridge to Buchanan. Our descent route from Carthew to the ridge included about 80 feet of class 4 rock. A belay there was a good precaution.

It was a 9 ½ hour trip from Cameron Lake to Waterton Townsite via the two peaks. There were spectacular ridge walks on our route.

Grinnell Point   7,600 ft.

Many Glacier area, Glacier National Park.

July 26, 1987. Our large Glacier Mountaineering Society group led by Dick Schwab and Gordon Edwards included Sarah, George, Denis, Shi, Karla, Diane, Chester, Art, Edward, Steve, Ann, Maggie, Carol and Carl.

From Swiftcurrent, we ascended the class 2 and 3 east ridge route via the Josephine mine, and descended the same route.

We looked in the old mine shaft and all agreed that it would not be wise to enter it. We reached the summit in 2 ½ hours from our starting point.

Beautiful weather, great views.

Mt. Pollack 9,211 ft.   Bishop's Cap 9,127 ft.

Logan Pass area, Glacier National Park.

August 9, 1987. The ascent route for our group of five climbers was from Lunch Creek to the east couloir on Pollack. Elevation gain was about 3,000 feet. Ascent time 1 ½ hours, and the route was easy with a bit of class 3 in a place or two. After reaching the summit of Pollack, we then took the ridge from Pollack on to Bishop's Cap via a descending traverse to the notch.

The final short pitch to the summit of Bishop's Cap is a narrow chute that affords a bit of easy rock climbing. The summit itself is small and narrow, and towers over a steep cliff on the northeast side.

After climbing Bishop's Cap, we descended by climbing down the chute above the Arches to the High Line trail. We were back at Lunch Creek in less than 8 hours for the round trip. Beautiful day. We saw Mountain Sheep and Goats on this climb.

Summits and Trails

Gary and Karla on the summit of Reynolds in Glacier Park. Going-to-the-Sun Mountain looms in the distance, with St. Mary Lake in the valley

The mountains surrounding Logan Pass, in Glacier Park, viewed from Bishop's Cap.

Summits and Trails

Mt. Clements   8,760 ft.

Logan Pass area, Glacier National Park.

On August 23, 1987, Denis, Chester, Dale, Becky, Jan, Sarah, Karla and I started from the Logan Pass parking lot and worked our way up toward the saddle between Clements and Oberlin. From there, we traversed across the face to the coulier, and ascended Clements by the east face couloir route.

The ascent to the summit took 2 hours and 20 minutes with an elevation gain of 2,008 feet. We had some class 4 climbing going up the steep couloir. Loose rock was a major hazard on the ascent, and we were very careful to not dislodge anything that might fall on those climbing below us. The weather was cool and nice, but the summit of the mountain became cloud covered, and the views from the top were obscured by the clouds.

We returned to the Logan Pass parking area by way of the normal route above Hidden Lake.

Triple Divide   8,020 ft.   Norris Mountain   8,882 ft.

Cut Bank area, Glacier National Park.

On August 30, 1987 Denis, Shi, Sarah, Jan, Karla and I left our camp at Cut Bank Creek Campground and took the trail to the east face of Triple Divide. At one point along the trail, Karla and I saw a large grizzly grazing on the slope below us. It paid no attention to us, and we made plenty of noise as we hurried on by. The others in our party were a bit ahead of us, and they did not see the bear when they passed this point on the trail.

The ascent time for our climb of Triple Divide was 2 ½ hours, and our route up to the summit was class 3 and 4. Elevation gain was 2,900 feet. Great weather.

We then went on to climb Norris via the south face, which gave us an additional 1,100 feet of class 3 and 4 climbing. That took 3 ½ hours. We descended via the same route, the couloir in the notch. The round trip time for both peaks from our camp was 12 hours.

At our tent sites in the Cut Bank campground the night before our climb we were energized by large helpings of Jan's delicious home-made lentil soup.

Mt. Rainier   14,400 ft.

Rainier National Park, Washington.

September 6 and 7, 1987. Members of our climbing party included Denis, Shi, Mark, Steve, Jan, Jaime, Karla, Bob and Brian. We used crampons, ice axes, rope, harness, and carabineers on this climb.

The day before our climb, we all took part in a refresher course in using our ice axes for self arrest. We were also taught the "rest step," a method of walking that works well at high altitude.

From Paradise Lodge, we hiked up past Camp Muir to the Ingraham Glacier where we made camp at 11,000 feet. We used our ice axes to chop level places in the glacial ice to pitch our tents.

We were up at 2:00 a.m. for breakfast and were ready to go by headlamp at 4:00 a.m.. We left our tents pitched at the campsite until our return. We roped up before leaving our camp, with Denis, Shi, Karla and I making up one rope team.

We experienced some bad rock fall in the darkness as we approached Disappointment Cleaver. Falling rocks of various sizes narrowly missed us. We could hear them crashing and ricocheting as they came tumbling down from high above us, and in the yellow light of our headlamps we watched them flying by. Fortunately no one was hurt

We climbed up the cleaver, and due to hazardous conditions on the normal route above Ingraham Glacier we traversed over to the Emmons Glacier and went on to the summit from there. At one point on the ascent above the Emmons Glacier, a passenger jet flew by the mountain, apparently on it's descent into the Seattle Tacoma airport, and we were actually above it, looking down on it as it flew by. We were on the summit at noon. Elevation gain from Paradise was 9,000 feet.

We descended the same route via the cleaver that we had gone up earlier. Back at our campsite, we packed up our tents and sleeping bags and continued on to Camp Muir and then on down the mountain.

Sun cups on Mt. Rainier.

Summits and Trails

Ice formations high on glacial slopes.

Climbers work their way up Mt. Rainier.

Summits and Trails

Sun cups on Mt. Rainier.

Rope team descending from the summit of Mt. Rainier.

Summits and Trails

Setting up camp on the Ingraham Glacier, Mt. Rainier.

It took us 17 ½ hours to climb from the lodge to the summit, and 11 hours from the summit back to our room at the lodge. We walked the last few miles in the dark of night, using our headlamps, and we were at the lodge by 11:30 p.m.. All were exhausted upon arrival back at Paradise. We decided that the next time we climbed this route, on our return we would stay another night at our camp on the Ingraham Glacier.

Mount Cannon   8,952 ft.

Logan Pass area, Glacier National Park.

September 20, 1987. Our party included Denis, Shi, Karla, Jan, Sarah, Sharon, Jerry and son. Our ascent route was along a goat trail that traversed the north face of Mount Clements to the saddle between Cannon and Clements. The route was class 3 and 4, and a short stretch of 5.4 around and above an impassable gully of sheer rock on the traverse across the north face of Clements. Most of us used a belay at this point.

After reaching the saddle between Clements and Cannon, we scrambled on up the narrow ridge to the summit of Cannon. Elevation gain was 2,200 feet. We agreed that this route is best done in the fall, to avoid steep snow fields.

Descent route was via the Hidden Lake trail. It took us 9 hours for the round trip.

Summits and Trails

Popocatepetl 17,887 ft.   **Iztaccihuatl** 17,343 ft.
El Pico de Orizaba 18,850 ft.

Mexico

December 24 - December 31, 1987.

    In Mexico City we were met by our three climbing guides and the other members of our group of seven climbers. Due to the serious altitude involved, and the logistics involved in climbing three peaks in two weeks, we had joined a group of climbers led by guides from the American Alpine Institute, from Bellingham, Washington. Thus we were assured not only of a chance at the three summits, but also of an opportunity to receive instruction in high altitude physiology and illnesses such as HAPE, HACE, and acute mountain sickness.
    We also received instruction on nutrition, acclimatization, efficient movement at altitude, and other climbing skills. After the climbs we felt confident in our ability to recognize and respond to high altitude illnesses.
    Although we had been exposed to much of the technical aspects of glacier travel on our climb of Rainier, such as French and German technique with crampons, ice axe self arrest, roped travel, and rope handling skills, we received additional training in these, and also did do some hands-on use of prusik slings, which is a valuable crevasse rescue technique.

A crevasse below the summit rim of Mt. Popocatepetl in Mexico.

Our instructor-guides, two men and a woman, had extensive experience as climbing guides in the Cascades, and Jeff. having been a climbing guide in Mexico for five years, really knew his way around. Jill had guided in Bolivia last year, and this would be her first climb in Mexico. Dave, the other guide, was also to have his first try at the volcanoes. They were, however, experienced climbers on both ice and rock.

The necessary qualifications for joining the group were that one needed to have had basic mountaineering experience combined with ice and snow climbing experience. One member of our group had climbed in Bolivia and India, as well as in the U.S.. Only one was inexperienced in climbing, a fellow from Long Island, who had trained long and hard by lifting weights, which put him at a decided disadvantage due to the excess muscle that required that much more oxygen. He succeeded in making the summit on the last (and highest) peak only by extreme effort. He did not summit on the first two.

There were two capable and experienced women with us beside Karla and Jill, the guide. One was from Billings, MT, and the other made her home in Miami. The group proved quite compatible, a good bunch to climb with.

We had our own harnesses, ice axes, carabineers, headlamps, packs, etc., and the Institute furnished the cooking utensils, stoves, ropes, other technical gear. We rented double boots, helmets, and crampons from the Institute.

On our way to Tlamacas, we stopped at the village of Amecameca where there was a large market place to buy food for the first two climbs. That in itself was quite an experience, with individual Mexicans and Indians having their wares spread out on blankets on the ground, or on improvised tables. The market was large, both indoor and outside, and you could find just about every kind of commodity imaginable. We stocked up on lots of fresh fruits, vegetables, pastas and home made breads, along with other items. Unfortunately, two members of our party got sick after drinking tea purchased in the market.

As for the altitude, when we reached our base at the lodge at Tlamacas at 12,800 feet, I had a headache and general malaise for about 72 hours while acclimatizing, even though we had spent 3 days in Mexico City at over 7,000 feet. The rapid ascent from 7,000 to 13,000 feet had all of us feeling rough for a few days.

Popocatepetl was our first peak, and a few hours before our ascent (which started at 1:30 a.m., by headlamp) my headache left. I did feel the altitude, but Jeff, one other climber and myself managed to make the summit at 17,887 feet. Karla, Robin, and two of our guides were forced to turn back at the edge of the glacier above the upper Ventorillo, or Queretano Hut, at about 16,400 feet.

Brian, Jeff, and I put on our crampons and continued on up to the summit. This climb up the north face involved about two and one half hours of glacier travel, most of it on steep and very hard ice. We arrived at the summit about 8 hours after we had left the lodge. It was a great, sunny and clear day. Looking down into the deep crater, which is about one half mile across, with almost vertical walls, we were rewarded with an awesome sight. We descended by a longer but easier route, and after leaving the glacier enjoyed a scree-type run down soft volcanic ash for several thousand feet.

Summits and Trails

Climbers ascending the Ayoloco Glacier, high on Mt. Itzaccihuatl in Mexico.

After a one day rest, we again got a very early start by headlamps and attempted Mt. Iztaccihuatl, a peak that is a sister peak to Popo, and just a few miles away across the Pass of Cortez. This mountain is also known as "sleeping lady" because of its profile. While it was the lesser of the three in altitude, reaching 17,343 feet, it proved to be the most interesting to climb, offering greater diversification of terrain to ascend and descend. When we reached the glacier we put on crampons and roped up. The group was becoming more acclimatized, and everyone in our party was able to make the summit. I felt much better on this climb, and Karla was able to summit with us. We could look over from the summit and see Popocatepetl, the mountain that we had just climbed two days before.

These two peaks required climbing from 4,500 to 5,000 feet vertical on the summit days, and time involved was twelve and fourteen hours each, with the descents being fairly rapid.

The next day we drove on back roads through several isolated and primitive Indian communities that have remained pretty much unaffected by modernization. After about a four hour drive we arrived in the city of Puebla, where we had a room in a centuries old hotel that at one time had been a monastery. After a few days rest and time spent enjoying the sights of the city (plus some great Mexican food, all very inexpensive) we drove to the small village of Tlachichuca.

On our arrival in Tlachichuca, a small farming village at the edge of the foothills below the mountain, we locate the man who is to drive us to the climbing hut. He lives in a small, neat and clean house surrounded by a tall, yellow adobe wall. He invites our group of eight climbers and three guides into his home to meet his wife and sign the climbing register, a large notebook containing hundreds of signatures of climbers from all over the world.

Back outside in the courtyard our gear is being loaded onto an ancient, black four wheel drive pickup truck that has a wooden stock rack on it. We put our packs as far to the front as possible, and when they are stacked to the top of the rack, place the remaining half dozen or so on top of the cab, where our driver lashes them down with a small rope.

While we are loading, people ride by on the dusty street in horse drawn carts and wagons, loaded high with firewood and dry yellow corn stalks. The icy summit of El Pico Orizaba, the third highest mountain in North America, looms above the horizon in the hazy distance, seeming very far away.

A shout from his wife takes the driver back into the house, and when he returns he has a look of concern. He informs us that there has been a climbing accident on Orizaba, and that we will be expected to assist in bringing down a body. He also says we should be prepared to spend the night with the body in camp if necessary. This announcement has a sobering effect on all of us, and I wonder what it will be like once we reach the climbing hut.

When everything is loaded to his satisfaction, our driver tells us to get aboard, and advises us to cover our mouths and noses with scarves or handkerchiefs as protection against the dust that we are sure to experience once we get under way. We go down the narrow street looking like a group of bandidos.

The street quickly turns into a rutted dirt road, and that in turn evolves into a narrow two-lane cow trail, bordered closely on each side by deep eroded gullies that threaten to swallow the struggling pickup should we slide into one.

Climbers ascending the Glaciar de Jamapa, on Mt. Orizaba in Mexico.

Descending into the clouds, from the summit of Orizaba.

The road forks often, and we go first right, then left, then right again. Fenced brown fields border the road on each side. Dust boils up behind the truck, and covers us with a fine powdery beige. Soon we start to climb, and after a long time we pass a small village located high on the wooded slopes. I want to stop for a closer look, but the truck makes a bouncing right turn, and continues grinding its tortuous way up the mountain.

The landscape is still tree covered, broken by grassy slopes and small cultivated fields along each side of the road. We have an occasional glimpse of small bands of sheep with their herders close by, and now and then someone on horseback appears, ambling off the trail and viewing us from the trees along the roadside. In a few more miles the fields disappear, and the old truck grinds its slow and bumpy way through scattered stands of dark green trees and layered rock.

Soon we emerge onto a high ridge covered with sparse brown grasses. Until now the sky had been overcast, but visibility was good. Now, however, as the mountain opens up before us, we can see that the summit is shrouded in clouds. At least the road is smoother, the dust has stopped being a problem, and it isn't long until we are in sight of the hut.

At 14,000 feet, nestled into the mountain side on a boulder strewn slope, the Piedra Grande hut is a one and one-half story building made of stone and concrete, with windows along one side and end, and topped with a peaked roof of corrugated metal. There is a spring a short distance away, its cold water flowing from the rocky hillside through a short length of moss covered pipe. There are several crosses and memorials just above the hut, with inscriptions in Spanish remembering those who have died on the mountain.

Summits and Trails

Inside, beneath the windows, a rustic cooking counter extends halfway along one wall, and wooden sleeping platforms extend from the full length of the opposite wall. The hut can hold over 50 people if sleeping bags are placed side by side. Fortunately, although it is the busy Christmas season, there is only one other party here, so we have no trouble finding a place for our food and equipment.

After we unload our gear, two of the guides and I volunteer to start up the mountain to meet the rescue party. We take ice axes, crampons and ropes, along with warm clothing and headlamps. Its getting dark fast, and we have no idea how far up the mountain we will have to go.

A narrow trail leads upwards from the hut, winding its way steeply through boulders and volcanic debris along the edge of a rocky gully, making the going difficult. We walk in silence for half an hour, each with his own thoughts, the route becoming steeper and narrower as we go. The mountain, the rock, the trail, all are in shades of somber gray. Clouds envelope us as we gain altitude.

The thin air forces us to go slow, and we settle into a familiar pace that allows us to move steadily without undue fatigue. After a while the clouds lift suddenly and we see people coming down the mountain toward us. We continue to make our way upward, and soon we can see the stretcher they are carrying. When we meet, the group is glad to see us, although few words are spoken.

The body on the litter is tied in place with straps of frayed brown webbing. Crampons are still attached to scuffed leather hiking shoes. Someone has tied a piece of torn cardboard over the face. We relieve three of the litter bearers, and retrace our steps back down the slope to the hut. The going is slow and torturous, the route narrow and winding. On arrival we are met by the others, who watch in silence as we place the body in the back of the waiting pickup. Most of the onlookers have cameras, but they stay in their cases, untouched. Someone announces that there is hot water for tea and cocoa, so we go inside the hut and pour drinks. Supper is cooking on two white gas stoves, and gas lanterns cast shadows on the rock walls as we warm our hands around cups of hot liquid.

    A woman climber that is with the other group is telling of her encounter with the dead man's climbing partner immediately after the accident. She and her friends had just reached the summit, and were starting back down when they encountered a man who was apparently in a state of shock. He related that a short distance below the summit, on their way down, he had called out to his friend, who was below him, "I think we should rope up now." His partner had answered yes, that in a couple of steps he would be in a good place to rope up. His next step was to be the last he would ever take.

    The man told her he watched as his friend slipped and tried desperately to self arrest with his ice axe. But the ice was too hard, and for fifty feet he rapidly gained momentum, his axe leaving faint scratch marks on the surface of the glacier. Finally his crampons caught in the ice, and he was thrown outward from the frozen face of the mountain. For 1,200 feet he slid and tumbled wildly down the glacier before his body finally came to a stop in the jagged rocks below the ice.

    The woman said they had tied the survivor into their rope team and brought him down, and then had sent word to the village that help was needed. Local Mexican climbers had responded and had assisted in locating the body.

    As we finished our hot drinks we heard the pickup leave for the long bumpy trip down the mountain in the darkness. I'm sure some of us were grateful to have the body of the climber gone. The next morning after breakfast we scramble about on the slopes near the hut for a few hours to help acclimatize for our summit attempt. The clouds of the previous day have disappeared, and the mountain is bathed in sunlight. From the front of the hut we can look up at the brilliant whiteness of the glacier below the summit of Orizaba. In the clear mountain air it looks nearer than it is. We will spend one more day taking short walks at this altitude, then on the third day we will attempt the summit.

At 1:30 a.m., on the morning of our third day at the hut, we climb sleepily down from our loft and prepare a breakfast of cereal, juice, coffee and tea. Two of our party stir a few spoonfuls of powdered Jell-O into a cup of hot water as the drink of choice, but this concoction is too sweet for my taste. I prefer tea with my hot oatmeal.

Breakfast over, those of us who expect blisters in the usual places apply tape and "Second Skin" to our feet. Packs that were readied the night before are now double checked, and water bottles and lunches are placed in their proper niches. We attach headlamps to our climbing helmets, as the first few hours of the climb will be in darkness. Stars shine brightly in the night sky as we start up the rocky draw that will take us to the glacier.

It is 2:00 a.m., and we are leaving on schedule. Boulders revealed in the soft yellow glow of our headlamps cast long black shadows as we work our way up the rocky slope. I watch the feet of the person ahead of me, looking for loose rock, and being careful not to dislodge any that could fall on those below. After an hour's climbing, one of our group turns back, unable to continue because of mountain sickness. He starts back alone, but we do not worry about him, as the going so far has been relatively easy.

At 16,000 feet we reach the foot of the Glacier de Jamapa just as the sun is casting its first light onto the mountain. To our right, at the edge of the glacier, the sheer rock face of El Sarcofago is bathed in gold as we stop to put on crampons and rope up.

Now two more climbers announce their decision to turn back. They have not acclimatized successfully. We discuss the fact that we are now at a critical point of our climb. From here on if anyone has to turn back, it will mean that the rest of his or her rope team will have to go back too. The glacier is too steep, and the ice too hard and slippery, to allow anyone to travel un-roped beyond here.

The seven of us that remain are confident that we can continue. The reason for our confidence is that we had climbed Popocatepetl and Iztaccihuatl the previous week. These peaks were at 17,750 and 17,350 feet, and although not all of us had made it to the summits, those climbs had served to acclimatize us well. The three that turned back had joined our group late, and had not participated in the two previous climbs. We felt that this lack of preparation had undoubtedly affected their performance today.

At least three hours of tedious climbing in oxygen thin air, and over 2,500 vertical feet of glacier lay ahead of us before we would gain the summit. We inch slowly but steadily upward, the sound of our labored breathing and crampons biting into hard ice is all we hear. The sky above remains a brilliant blue, but as we climb we can see a thick layer of silver gray clouds gathering around the mountain below us. Above the cotton-like clouds we can see the blue shadow of Orizaba's summit reaching out towards the western horizon.

We seem to be living in a world of slow motion, where every move is deliberate. Surrounded by the white ice and snow of the glacier, our two rope teams use the rest step and pressure breathing to help alleviate the effect of the high altitude. I am feeling very well, and think that I could go faster if necessary, but when attached to others by a rope, the team moves only as fast as the slowest member can manage. I realize that our pace is a good one, and that it would be foolish to try to go faster. After our climb I learn that some reached the summit only by extending their determination and will power to their limit.

As we climb, I recall the time a few years ago when, having flown to 17,000 feet as a passenger in a light plane, I passed out because of lack of oxygen. That incident was the result of a rapid ascent and a faulty oxygen mask. Now I am climbing at over 18,000 feet, and feeling very strong. At last we reach the rocks at the rim of the crater.

Just a little further now, and we will be at just under 19,000 feet, on top of the third highest peak in North America. As we approach the top, we can see the large iron crosses that have been placed on the summit in memory of those who met with tragedy on this mountain. It is difficult to imagine how anything bad could happen in such a beautiful place, but the sight of thick clouds gathering below brings us back to reality, and after some quick photos and congratulatory handshakes and hugs, we head back down the glacier.

Five hundred feet below the summit we enter the clouds, and it becomes difficult to see the other members of our rope team. We know we could be in trouble if visibility does not improve soon, as there are places where getting off route could mean disaster. But instead of improving, it gets worse. Now I cannot see the man ahead of me, only a few feet of rope leading off into a gray mist. There are no tracks for the leader to follow, as the ice is too hard for our crampons to have left any trace of our passing. We will have to stop and wait, and hope that this cloud cover lifts soon.

We feel a welcome breeze on our faces, and with it comes a feeling of relief as we start to make out other members of our party. Then, like the opening of a curtain on a giant stage, the clouds lift and we recognize landmarks below us that tell us we are on the correct route.

Soon we are at the foot of the glacier, where we unrope and remove our crampons. From here we have but to follow the rocky ridge until we can drop down into the ravine that leads to the hut.

Although we are tired, the feeling of accomplishment that we had at the summit is still with us. The memory of today will stay with us all our lives. While our route had not been technically difficult, the hard steep ice and the high altitude had combined to present us with a challenging climb. The victim of the climbing accident had made us all well aware of the risk, and we knew how much could be lost should anything go wrong. Yet our group of ordinary people had reached beyond their ordinary lives to find something we hoped we had within ourselves, and although we perhaps could not name this thing we searched for, we knew we had found it.

Summits and Trails

* * * * *

I know a changing place,
where hills of shifting sand
are forever moving,
covering fences and homesteads
and meadows.

Driven by relentless winds
that fly through the high passes
and sweep across the sage covered land,
and the wind driven sand stings
and cuts your face and hands

* * * * *

Mad Wolf 8,341 ft. **Eagle Plume** 8,724 ft.
Bad Marriage 8,350 ft.

Cut Bank area of Glacier National Park.

June 26, 1988. A three peak ridge walk circuit, class 3 most of the way. Ken, Karla, Rob, Jan and Bill were in our party on a windy and overcast day. We saw mountain sheep and lots of wild flowers. Total elevation gain was about 3,200 feet. There was about 3 miles of ridge walk on our route.

Karla sprained her ankle at the falls area on the way down from the last summit. Fortunately, I had some elastic bandage in the first aid kit in my pack, and we wrapped her ankle so she could walk. The round trip from our starting point to and back took eleven hours.

Mt. Boswell 7,874 ft.

Waterton Park, Canada.

July 3, 1988. Sunny and cool. Denis, Shi, Jan, Karla and I, after taking a boat from Waterton townsite to a point south of Crypt Landing, ascended the west ridge of Boswell via 2 bands of cliffs that afforded high class 4 and low class 5 climbing. On our ascent we saw mountain sheep and goats.

Our descent route was southeast from the summit to a beautiful pond below Crypt Lake. From there we hiked on down to Waterton Lake. There was lots of bear grass in bloom on this trip. A great climb in beautiful weather.

Sinopah   8,271 ft.

Two Medicine area, Glacier National Park.

July 17, 1988. This climb was with a very large group, but it was fun to do and the weather was great. We ascended the south east face of the mountain. There was lots of good rock in the gully that we went up.

About 2,700 feet of elevation gain to the summit, with some steep class 3 climbing. Sinopah is a much photographed mountain and a prominent feature in the Two Medicine area. From the top we looked down on Two Medicine Lake, and in the distance we could see the large expanse of plains east of the mountains.

Mt. Henkel   8,770 ft.

Many Glacier area Glacier National Park.

July 24, 1988. Gordon Edwards, Dick Schwab, Denis, Shi, Ann, Vic, Jackie and I climbed up the south couloir and came back down the same route. Class 2 and 3 with an elevation gain of 4,000 feet. We were 3 hours going up, 1 ½ on summit, 1 ½ down.

There was some good rock in the long gully on our ascent and descent. Like all mountains in the park, the views from the summit were well worth the climb.

Mt. Merritt   10,004 ft.

Belly River area, Glacier National Park.

July 28, 29, 30, 1988. Den, Shi, Brett, Sarah, Carl, Karla and I backpacked 14 miles from Chief Mountain customs station to Mokowanis junction campground on Saturday. This is a very scenic area of the park. A few hours after we had set up our tents, a moose walked through our camp while we were there. It did not pay any attention to us. There were also deer in our campground from time to time.

Beautiful weather for all three days. We climbed on Sunday and came out on Monday. We took the ridge above Old Sun Glacier that led to the summit and avoided getting out on the glacier. Class 3 and 4 with an elevation gain of 4,600 feet. The ascent took us 5 hours. We were back down in half that time, after spending 30 minutes on the summit enjoying the views.

The views from the summit were fantastic. Distant hanging valleys, waterfalls, mountain peaks and spectacular scenery in every direction.

Summits and Trails

Old Sun Glacier, high on Mt. Merritt, Glacier National Park.

Mt. Wilbur 9,321 ft.

Many Glacier area of Glacier National Park.

August 13, 1988. Karla, Denis, Shi, Jan and I left the Swiftcurrent area at 8:00 a.m., and ascended the east face direct (overhang) route. The upper 500 feet is mostly class 4 and 5 pitches. At 3:00 p.m., after 7 hours of climbing and 4,500 feet of elevation gain we reached the summit. From there, we had a spectacular view of Iceberg Lake which is nestled far below the summit of the mountain.

We had two rappels on the way down, and we belayed several times on both ascent and descent. Lots of loose rock. We were thankful for our climbing helmets. The descent took us 8 hours. We made it down below the cliffs just before dark. We came back down the lower slopes and trail via headlamp and flashlight, making lots of noise to alert any bears that might have been nearby.

Mt. Wilbur is one of the 5 technical peaks in Glacier Park.

Summits and Trails

Mt. Wilbur, high above Iceberg Lake, Glacier National Park.

Mt. Adams   12,276 ft.

Washington Cascades.

September 2, 3, 4, 1988. Jan, Karla and I camped 2 nights at about 8,500 feet on a lava rock ridge on the lower slope of the mountain. We had a good climb, at a leisurely pace on our class 1 and 2 route. Our ascent route was up the south spur, and our descent route was the same. There was about 6,000 feet total elevation gain.

There were many other climbers on the mountain. The day was sunny, but hazy from the smoke of distant forest fires. There were many interesting sun cups and ice formations on the upper snow field below the summit. Beautiful ice formations below the summit. There was also lots of lava rock. After reaching the top, we had fun glissading down a snowfield on our way back down the mountain.

Pigeon Spire   10,250 ft.

Bugaboo Range, Canada.

October 8, 9, 10, 1988. Den, Shi, Karla and I hiked into the Conrad Kain hut (a great hut!) with full packs and spent 2 nights there. The trail up to the hut is a scenic climb in itself. At one point there is a ladder bolted to the face of a cliff which one must climb up, and then there is a fixed cable along one particularly narrow stretch of trail along the side of a steep, rock slope. A wonderful and scenic area, miles of glaciers and snow fields dotted with tremendous granite peaks.

Summits and Trails

A climber high on the slopes of Mt. Adams.

Snow and ice formations on Mt. Adams.

Summits and Trails

The Howser Spires in the Bugaboos - Canada.

Snow Patch Spire in Canada's Bugaboos.

On the route up to Pigeon Spire, Bugaboos, Canada.

Bugaboo Glacier - Canada.

On the 9th, after climbing up a steep, snow filled couloir that flanks one side of the Bugaboo Spire, and then across a spectacular. glacier, we were able to ascend the west ridge of Pigeon Spire to the first of its 2 highest points, at about (a guess) 9,900 feet. There was a patch of ice and snow on the ridge between the 2 highest points, and as it was late in the day we felt we did not have enough time for belaying, so we turned back.

The climbing hut is a Quonset style building, and the Canadians helicopter in propane tanks to fuel the stoves in the kitchen. On the second floor is a dormitory type area where climbers can spread their sleeping bags. This is one of the most beautiful alpine areas I have ever been in. Wonderful rock, awesome spires and fantastic scenery. We all vowed to return to this wonderful area sometime in the near future.

Calf Robe   8,800 ft.

Marias Pass, Glacier Park.

October 23, 1988. On a stormy and overcast day, our group of five climbers turned back without making it to the summit because of very poor visibility on the mountain.

On our way up the mountain, at about 7,000 to 7,500 feet, we walked to within about 150 yards of two huge silvertip grizzlies before we spotted them. They were moving slowly in a westerly direction and they gave no indication that they saw us. The wind was blowing from them to us, which could have saved the day for us! One never knows what a grizzly bear's reaction to visitors might be.

They were beautiful, fat, bears. This close encounter in such poor visibility was another factor in our decision to turn back.

Mt. Stanton 7,750 ft.

Glacier Park, McDonald Creek area.

December 31, 1988. This was one of our annual, GMS, New Year's Eve climbs of Stanton. There were 10 climbers in our group. Some of us used X-country skis, and some were on snowshoes. It was a very tough climb in deep snow, but also very beautiful. The trees were all encased in snow and ice. The weather on the narrow summit was bitter cold, with blowing spindrift. The summit was a peak of snow with cornices on either side, and the ridge that continued on to Mt. Vaught was just a knife edge of drifted deep snow.

We spent the final four hours of our descent skiing by headlamp. Those of us who had them used our skis every bit of the way up and down. The snow was too deep and soft for the Sherpa snowshoes that a few of the climbers had with them. This climb was a great way to end the year!

Dragon's Tail viewed from the summit of Mt. Reynolds, Glacier National Park.

Grizzly Mountain   9,067 ft.

Two Medicine area, Glacier National Park.

June 18, 1989. Bill, Karla, myself and 3 others climbed Grizzly as the first climb of the season. It is about 6 hours from Two Medicine campground to the summit of Grizzly, much of it by trail. There was still quite a lot of snow on the trail in the Painted Tepee and Cobalt Lake area. The distance from the Two Medicine campground to the summit is about 11 miles.

As is true of all of the summits in the park, the views from the summit of Grizzly are well worth the effort.

Mt. Alderson   8,800 ft.

Waterton Park, Canada.

July 2, 1989. On a cold and clear day, Chester, Denis, Shi, Jan, Karla and I left Cameron Lake at about 8:00 a.m. bound for the summit of Alderson. The ascent was not difficult, but our descent route was via the south face, and we decided that it might have been a new route down the south face. It required 2 belays, one of which was over snow. We arrived back at Waterton Townsite via Bertha Lake, at about 6:00 p.m..

Flinsch Peak 9,225 ft.

Two Medicine area, Glacier National Park.

July 9, 1989. The sky was overcast when Karla, Sandi, Kathleen, Dan, Jason, and I left the trail head at Two Medicine at 7:45 a.m. and started up the trail to Dawson Pass. At the pass, we left the trail and climbed the south face to the summit of Flinsch. Weather was unusually cold for July, and we were surprised to find that the water in our water bottles had turned to ice.

Clouds lifted as we gained the summit, allowing good views in all directions. Our route to the summit was all class 2 and 3. We were back to our starting point at the trail head at 4:30 p.m..

Gary Yates

* * * * *

I know a lonely
far away place where there is
a huge partly hidden log
of green and blue
that time has turned to crystal.

The rings of a life
that once was a tree
are easily seen
and can be counted.

I know a little used trail
that traces a faint line
beside a whispering stream
as it flows below a mountain pass.

* * * * *

Summits and Trails

Mt Stanton 7,750 ft.

Lake McDonald area, Glacier National Park.

July 16, 1989. The weather was cloudy, but clearing as the day progressed. It was the first time up Stanton for Karla and Jan, and my third climb to the summit. We followed the same route that I had used on previous climbs, starting at the trail near the head of Lake McDonald and which leads up and over Howe Ridge

The elevation gain from the trail head was 4,550 feet. Class 2 and 3. An enjoyable but physically demanding climb.

Just a few feet below the summit, a mountain goat joined us for lunch. It approached quite near to us, and watched for a while as we ate our sandwiches. We didn't offer it anything, so it soon left us, heading off in the direction of Mt. Vaught. I did take a photo of it before it left.

Going-to-the-Sun Mt. 9,642 ft.

St. Mary Valley area, Glacier National Park.

August 13, 1989. A very large party of 21 climbers included Karla, Sandi, Bill, Larry, Arnold, Trevor, Caleb, Andy, Donald, Rob, Jason, Bill, Chris, George, Duz, Vic, Mehdi, Dan, Julie and Danny. This was one of many Glacier Mountaineering Society climbs that we did in the park. With a group of this size, rock fall becomes a major hazard and everyone was very careful not to dislodge any rocks on climbers below.

No matter how careful one is, however, sometimes rocks are dislodged, and the cry of, "rock!" can be heard from those on the route above. In the interest of safety the GMS members have discussed limiting the number of climbers on each climb. This will no doubt become a rule in the not too distant future.

Starting at Siyeh Bend, we went up the west face route, which presented an elevation gain of about 3,700 feet. Our route was class 3 with some class 4 pitches in the cliffs. Above the cliffs, we avoided the diagonal and instead scrambled up the scree slope to the summit.

Beautiful weather today, but a heavy rainfall the previous night had made wet rocks in the cliff band somewhat difficult. Several of the climbers used a belay in the cliff area.

On our approach to the mountain we saw a grizzly bear, several goats and 1 golden eagle. This was my second ascent of this mountain. After signing the register, and taking summit photos, we made our way back down the mountain by the same route we had taken going up.

Mountain Goat on the summit of Mt. Stanton, Glacier National Park.

St. Mary Lake from the summit of Going-to-the-Sun Mt. in Glacier National Park.

Summits and Trails

Grand Teton   13,766 ft.

Teton National Park, Wyoming.

September 3, 4, 5, 1989. Denis, Shi, Karla and I, camped 2 nights at the lower saddle at 11,200 feet. On summit day, Karly volunteered to stay at our camp and guard our tents against marmot raids.

We climbed on summit day mostly in rock climbing shoes. We climbed the Exum route, up Wall Street, then to the Friction Pitch and on up to the summit. There were several class 4 and 5 pitches. It took us 8 hours to reach the summit from our camp.

We descended via the Owen-Spalding route. We did 2 rappels on the descent, one about 60 feet, and one was 120 feet with 80 feet of it free, away from the cliff.

On our return, Karla told us what had happened with the marmots while we were gone. While a couple of them kept Karla distracted by performing antics on a nearby rock, some others crept behind Denis and Shi's tent and chewed a hole in it. Unseen by Karla, they went inside and made quite a mess of Denis and Shi's sleeping bags.

We spent another night in camp before starting back down to the valley floor where we had left our vehicles. A fun, classic climb with plenty of exposure and steep rock. Great weather.

Crescent Spire   9,350 ft.

Bugaboos, Canada.

September 16, 1989. Karla and I hiked in and spent a couple of nights at the Conrad Kain hut.

This was a solo climb for me. I left the Crescent-Eastport Col at 4:00 p.m., then climbed to the Crescent - Brenta Col. I ascended the NE ridge. It was a relatively short trip from the hut, and it only took 1 hour and 40 minutes to reach the summit. An elevation gain of about 2,000 feet.

It was interesting climbing on the ridge. There was no snow on the entire route. There are great cliffs below the summit but the narrow route felt protected. The worst part was the scramble up to the col on loose rock and fine scree. After a brief few minutes on the summit, and taking a couple of photos, I descended the same route I had climbed. I was back to the hut in 1 hour and 20 minutes, where Karla had a great meal waiting.

On the trail up to our base camp for our climb of the Grand Teton - Wyoming.

Bugaboo Glacier - Canada.

Summits and Trails

Piegan Mountain 9,230 ft.

Logan Pass area, Glacier National Park.

July 1, 1990. A class 2 scramble. There were 10 climbers in our group. Piegan was free of snow on the route up from Lunch Creek.

After reaching the summit of Piegan, we went on to Pollack. Ascending Pollack, due to deep snow on the route, we had to use 2 ropes as a fixed line in climbing up the couloir. Leaving the summit of Pollack, we went on to climb Bishop's Cap.

We then went down to the Highline trail, which was not officially open yet due to large amounts of snow, and back to Logan Pass. From there we went on to Lunch Creek where we had left our vehicles.

Mt. Joffre 11,300 ft.

Elk Lakes region, Canadian Rockies.

July 8, 1990. Denis, Brett, Shi, Karla and I backpacked for about 4 ½ hours from the Elk Lakes trail head into the Petain Basin. After working our way along a mountain lake and then following a creek for a while, we climbed some steep trails to get there, where we set up our camp. It is a beautiful place. We had 2 porcupines in camp that evening. A Canadian ranger had earlier confirmed our route from the

Petain Basin to Joffre.

Karla spent a leisurely day in camp. The rest of us set out fairly early on a beautiful morning and were on the glacier 1 ½ hours before reaching a saddle beyond the glacier where Shi decided to wait for us. The view to the north from that saddle was fantastic, with snow capped peaks as far as we could see.

There was lots of loose rock and soft snow. Our route was steep, up a snowfield to a narrow ridge about 3 feet wide that was covered with deep snow, with huge cornices and lots of exposure on each side. Our route was finally blocked by a cornice about 100 yards from a false summit of Joffre. We decided that to go further was not worth the risk, as there were avalanches all around us.

We turned back, and had a steep but pleasurable descent on snow and down very steep slopes. We were very leery of the small avalanches and frequent rock slides. Shi was waiting patiently for us at the saddle at the edge of the glacier. We worked our way back across the glacier and climbed down the rock cliffs above our camp site. We considered ourselves fortunate to have returned to camp unscathed.

It was indeed an adventure, and we all felt that we had made a wise decision to turn back when we did, even though we had been tantalizingly close to the summit.

A steep pitch on the descent from the attempt of Mt. Joffre - Canada.

Bear Grass high in the Rocky Mountains.

Mt. Brown   8,541 ft.

Lake McDonald area, Glacier National Park.

July 15, 1990. Karla and I started from near the Lake McDonald lodge and took the steep trail that switchbacks to the fire lookout high on the ridge. Karla stayed at the lookout while I went on to the summit. I was happily surprised to find that the ridge soon becomes very interesting rock climbing. It is good rock and fun to climb. After reaching the summit, I returned by going down into the east gully, then back to the ridge above the fire lookout, avoiding the rocky ridge.

We had a wonderful day on the mountain. Elevation gain 5,300 feet.

Mt. Kapunkamint   8,735 ft.

Cut Bank Creek area, Glacier National Park.

August 19, 1990. On a rainy day, with visibility limited to 100 feet or less at times, our group of nine climbers ascended the long west ridge leading to the summit. It took 5 ½ hours of class 2 and 3 climbing to gain 3,400 feet in elevation.

Karla spotted a grizzly when the weather lifted momentarily. We had seen a moose earlier, before starting our climb. Because of the rain, there was lots of slippery rock to contend with as we descended the same way we had gone up. Because of the limited visibility, we were apprehensive about the grizzly that we had seen earlier in the day, but we did not see it again.

Split Mountain   8,792 ft.

Cut Bank and St. Mary Valley area, Glacier National Park.

September 2, 1990. Denis, Shi, Karla and I took the trail from Cut Bank campground to Triple Divide Pass, where Karla waited for our return. We walked through an area that was carpeted with beautiful wild flowers as we crossed the glacial moraine to the Blueing Lake area and then traversed around to the west side of the summit formation. We then climbed the northern notch up around a chock stone, then followed a crack to a ledge below the summit.

From there we went on to the summit which we reached about 7 hours after leaving our camp. It was class 4 and 5 climbing on the summit formation, and the elevation gained was 2,400 feet. Falling rock was a great hazard, and we found it necessary to rappel twice on the way down.

Karla had watched our progress through binoculars, and on our return to the pass she told us that shortly after we had left the trail we had narrowly missed walking into a group of 4 grizzlies that were playing and feeding on the meadow area just over a slight rise from where we were crossing the moraine at the start of our climb.

She had wanted to warn us, but we were too far away. We

felt lucky that we did not walk right into them.

Pumpelly Pillar   7,600 ft.

Two Medicine area, Glacier National Park.

September 16, 1990. Cool and sunny day. Denis and I went up from the pond below upper Two Medicine Lake to a class 4 gully, then along a goat trail at line of trees to the eastern end of the ridge, then up a narrow chimney to the base of a split in the ridge. Then we angled to the left (west) to gain the ridge. A belay was necessary on the last short pitch. I climbed up and over an overhang which I could have avoided had I stayed just a bit to the right of my chosen route.

Our route to the summit consisted of some class 4 and 5 climbing on surprisingly good rock. There was no cairn on the summit, so we made a small one and placed a film canister in it with our names and the date. Descending we set up rappels for 7 pitches, including one rappel of 150 feet. We had left the trail head at 7:00 a.m. and we returned at 11:30 p.m, glad that we had headlamps with us.

One is always nervous about hiking in grizzly country after dark. I always try to avoid doing this, but once in a while it becomes necessary. I keep the pepper spray handy just in case.

We decided that this was a probable first ascent of Pumpelly Pillar by this route.

Climber on a narrow ridge between Summit Mt. and Little Dog Mt. in Glacier National Park.

Pumpelly Spire, Glacier National Park.

Mt. St. Nicholas   9,376 ft.

South Central Glacier National Park.

July 6, 1991. Denis, Shi, Karla and I backpacked 2 days (1 long and 1 short) in to the base of Mt. St. Nicholas, starting from Walton R.S. and on to Park Creek, up Park to Coal Creek, up Coal to Muir Creek crossing, then a tough bushwhack up Muir Creek to establish base camp near the foot of the falls below No-Name lake. In trying to avoid some bushwhacking, we took a wrong route up from the west side of Muir Creek, and after reaching the top of a long ridge we decided to spend the night there. The next day it was only a few more hours of hiking to where we set up our base camp. We had the whole afternoon to relax around camp, and rest up for the climb.

The next morning Denis, Shi and I ascended the snowy route to the Great Notch. Then we climbed class 5 pitches up the NE ridge to the top. There was lots of exposure on the route, and we certainly kept our minds on our climbing. It took us 9 hours and 20 minutes to reach the top from camp. After taking some summit photos, and signing the summit register, we did 8 or 9 rappels on our descent as we went down roughly the same route we had climbed.

Next day, we had a 10 hour hike back to trail head. As we were going down Muir Creek we encountered a grizzly with 2 cubs that were heading up the creek. We and the bears had entered a small clearing at the same time. We stopped, and the sow and cubs also stopped. They stood on their hind legs and looked at us, then turned and scurried back into the brush. Needless to say, we made a lot of noise the rest of the way out. The weather was great for the whole trip.

Little Dog 8,610 ft. **Summit** 8,770 ft.

Marias Pass area, Glacier National Park.

August 15, 1992. Our mixed group of twelve men and women left the parking area at 7:30 a.m. and took the direct route to the saddle on the ridge between the two peaks. At 11:15 a.m., we were on the saddle and on top of Summit at noon. We were back to the saddle at 1:00. and from there we climbed the short distance to the summit of Little Dog. We were back to the saddle at 2:10. We were down to our vehicles at 4:30 p.m..

Some clouds, but the temperatures were cool to warm and we had overall good weather. A little over 3,500 feet elevation gain. Class 2, 3, 4, and a short class 5 pitch on the route we chose. There was a mountain goat just below the ridge on our way up.

On a previous climb of Summit, which I did alone, I was very surprised to see the unmistakable tracks of a rabbit and a coyote on the crusted snow at the summit. Since both were traveling the same route, it appeared that the coyote might have been chasing the rabbit. I will never understand why either of them were up there, or how they got there, as it is a high, narrow and barren ridge. It was snow covered, and there was no reason for them to be there that I could see. A strange couple of climbing partners, to say the least.

Blackfoot Mt.   9,597 ft.

St. Mary Valley, Glacier National Park.

September 4, 5, 6, 7, 1992. Karla and Damon were not feeling well and stayed in camp at the foot of Jackson Glacier. Denis, Shi, Jeff, Dan and I climbed to the summit. We ascended via the Blackfoot Glacier route. Elevation gain was 4,900 feet, class 3, 4, and 5. The ascent took 7 hours, the descent took 6 hours.

On our planned summit day, the weather was broken, with intermittent periods of sun, wind and snow. The weather at daybreak was not good, but then after we had our breakfast it showed signs of clearing. We decided to go ahead with our climb, and we got a late start at 9:00 a.m.. There were frequent snow squalls throughout the day. During our ascent we set some wands on the glacier to help find our way back. Those were helpful on our return. It was snowing when we got back to our camp by head lamp at 11:00 p.m..

Blackfoot Mountain is one of Glacier National Park's 5 recognized technical climbs.

* * * * *

*Yellow and gray rock
forms steep walls
along the canyon sides.*

*One evening,
as a golden sun was touching
the distant horizon,
a silver cloud descended,
filling the canyon,
breaking the white light
into a spectrum of colors
that splashed about in the air
like paints spilled
from an artist's pallette.*

* * * * *

Santa Fe Baldy   12,622 ft.

Santa Fe Range, northern New Mexico.

June 8, 1993. I climbed this mountain alone on a clear and sunny day. There was a cold wind on top. It was about a 10 mile round trip from the Santa Fe ski basin and 2,000 feet of elevation gain. Nothing harder than a short stretch of class 4 along a rocky ridge. There was a snow cornice on top and snow on the route in many places. Lake Katherine, just below the summit, reminded me a bit of Iceberg Lake in Glacier Park in Montana. Great view from the summit. There are forests of fir and aspen below the peak.

I saw a few marmots and a mountain bluebird. It was a 7 hour round trip, and I was tired when I got back to "old blue," my pickup.

Lake Peak   12,409 ft.   Penitente Mt.   12,249 ft.

Santa Fe Range, Pecos Wilderness, New Mexico.

June 16, 1993. I did this class 2 and 3 route by myself. I hiked up the ski run to the ridge, then on to the summit of Lake Peak. It was a nice day, cool and sunny. I found 6 quarters, 1 ski cap and 1 earring as I hiked up beneath the lifts from the ski basin. A short hike, but 1,845 feet of elevation gain.

Ten days later, on the 26^{th,} there were still drifts of snow on the high ridges when Karla and I climbed this route together. Karla went with me up to the top and this time Karla found 7 quarters beneath the lifts. Walking up beneath ski lifts after snow melts is a bit like a treasure hunt.

From the summit of Lake Peak, we then took the short route over to the summit of Penitente. We saw a few big horn sheep on our way down from Penitente. A wonderful day.

We came back via the Winsor Trail. Seven hours in all on this climb.

Mt. Walton   8,926 ft.

St. Mary Valley area, Glacier National Park.

August 6, 7, 8, 1993. I flew from Santa Fe to Montana for this one and rented a car at the Kalispell airport. Denis, Shi and I backpacked in from the parking area on the Going-to-the-Sun Road. After a 4 hour hike, we set up our camp in a grassy area about 400 yards above the end of the spur trail from Gunsight campground.

On summit day we got a good start at 6:30 a.m.. It was very foggy but it soon lifted and the day became sunny and clear. Our route took us over the Harrison Glacier and the Jackson Glacier. Our route across the glaciers was long, we were 45 minutes on Jackson and 1 hour and 45 minutes on Harrison Glacier. Soft snow on the glaciers caused our crampons to ball up.

The mountain itself is quite steep to climb, class 4 and 5 and 3,600 feet of elevation gain. After reaching the summit we down-climbed the third couloir and then did one rappel to reach the traverse position. It was about a 16 hour round trip from our camp to the summit and back. We saw a goat on the mountain.

We reached our camp area at 10:30 p.m., shortly after dark. It had become very foggy, and we had difficulty locating our food cache and our tents by the light from our head lamps.

We discovered that some rodents had chewed their way into Denis' and Shi's food cache while we were away from camp, and ate a small amount of their supply.

We were finally in our sleeping bags around midnight. The next day, after a leisurely breakfast, we packed up our tents and left our campsite at 10:00 a.m., and were back to the Going-to-the-Sun Road at 2:10 p.m..

We all missed having Karla with us, as this climb was the final successful climb of all of Glacier's 5 technical peaks for the All-Bran team of Denis, Shi, Karla and me!

Wheeler Peak 13,161 ft.

Sangre de Cristo Mountains, New Mexico.

September 5, 1993. Karla and I backpacked a steep 2 miles from the trailhead to Bull-of-the-Woods meadow and set up our camp in a nice spot in the trees above the meadow. It was a 3 hour hike from the camp to the summit. Class 2 all the way.

It was a Labor Day weekend climb, and the weather was clear and sunny. There were lots of hikers on this one. We chose a somewhat different route for our descent, one which led along a rocky ridge for a ways and to a gully that we descended to the meadow.

Wheeler is the highest mountain in New Mexico, and from the summit we could see some of the many snow-capped peaks in Colorado.

South Truchas   13,102 ft.   **Middle Truchas**   13,066 ft.

Sangre de Cristo Mountains, Truchas region, New Mexico.

July 3, 1994. Karla and I drove on a terrible 4 WD road from the village of Truchas to the trail head. There was only room for 3 vehicles to park. We hiked roughly 4 miles to some falls, then another 30 minutes to where we camped at the amphitheater at about 11,500 feet. It is a beautiful area, the weather was cool, and there were still some snow drifts in places, including just behind our campsite.

We climbed up through a scree slope in the Truchas amphitheater, and on the way we saw lots of wild flowers and some big horn sheep with their young. After some more climbing we reached the summit of Middle Truchas, and then followed the ridge ½ mile to the summit of South Truchas.

A great climb, with some rock on the descent between Middle Truchas and the saddle above Truchas Lakes. This climb compared favorably with some that we had done in the mountains in Montana, and the rock that we experienced was good and solid for the most part. The summit was only about a 5 hour round trip from our camp. Our route was class 3 and 4.

Cerro Pedernal   9,862 ft.

Santa Fe National Forest, New Mexico.

August 6, 1994. A short climb, with an elevation gain of 1,860 feet. Karla and I drove up past Lake Abiquiu to Youngsville, then drove south for 5 miles to a meadow at 8,000 feet. Then we climbed 3 miles east and northeast through the woods to the base, and went up through a break in the cliff on the west side of the mountain.

Cerro Pedernal is Spanish for "Flint Mountain." The mountain was a source for chalcedony and agate used by Indians for arrowheads, spear points, knives, etc. Our route was class 3 through the cliff, the rest was class 2. We had wonderful views of Lake Abiquiu, red rock canyons, and the surrounding forest.

It was about a 3 ½ hour round trip from where we parked. We talked about spending a moonlight night camping on the summit sometime. Because of its shape and the narrow summit ridge, the mountain reminded us a bit of Chief Mt. in Montana.

Summits and Trails

Hope Mt.   13,012 ft.

Weminuche Wilderness, San Juan Mountains, Colorado.

September 1, 1994. Karla and I were on a backpacking trip of several days in length. We got on the narrow gauge steam train in Durango and took a scenic ride toward Silverton to where we and some other hikers were dropped off at a trail in the mountains. Today, which is the next to the last day of our hike, we barely got the tent up at our campsite at 11,000 feet before we got hit with a hail storm. That storm did not last long, and after we ate, Karla explored the area above camp and checked out some old mine shafts.

While she was doing that, I took a short hike up Hope Mt., just above camp. I went up Johnson Creek., then up to the summit, and then down the north ridge. The elevation gain from our camp was about 600 feet, and route was class 3. The ridge was narrow and fun, with a straight drop into Hazel Lake cirque.

The next morning we went over Columbine Pass, then on down the drainage about 9 miles to the railroad tracks. We got there in time to flag down the narrow gauge train for a ride back to Durango.

On a backpacking trip in Colorado's San Juan Mountains.

Mt. Monadnock   3,165 ft.

New Hampshire.

August 6, 1995. Karla and I climbed the rocky trail to the summit on a beautiful day. About 2,000 feet of elevation gain. There was a terrific wind on top and we were glad that we had our Goretex parkas with us. We had great views from the summit. We have heard that this mountain is possibly the most climbed mountain in North America, although we met only a few other people on our climb.

Mt. Mansfield   4,393 ft.

Vermont.

August 23, 1995. I climbed Mansfield, Vermont's highest mountain, on a sunny day. The route I chose was a relatively easy hike up it, with only a small elevation gain. There was a light wind, and it was cool on top. My parka felt good. From the summit I could see the Green Mountains, White Mountains. and the Adirondacks.

Mt. Marcy   5,244 ft.

Adirondack Mountains, New York.

September 23, 1995. Karla and I backpacked to Marcy Lake where we set up our tent and camped 2 nights. Mt.

Marcy is the highest mountain in New York State. Beautiful weather, leaves were turning color, and it was a fun climb. There was a trail almost all the way to the summit. From the top we had great views of the Adirondacks.

There were several other climbers and hikers on the trail, as this is a very popular area.

Ben Nevis   4,406 ft.

Scotland, United Kingdom.

October 21, 1995. Karla and I took the standard, regular route to the summit. Class 2 and 3. It was warm and sunny below the high saddle. There was ice in places on the trail, and it was windy and cold, but sunny on the summit. We had been warned that fast changing weather is very much a possibility on Ben Nevis. It took us 3 hours and 20 minutes to the summit, 3 hours descent time. The summit is 4,406 feet above sea level from the shore of Lock Linnhe, so the elevation gain on the climb was significant. There were some interesting items at the cairn on the summit. One was a rock from Mt. Everest, courtesy of Sir Edmund Hillary.

On our return to Fort William, we had dinner of "bangers and mash," and a pint of ale at Ben Nevis Bar and Restaurant, and afterwards we went to a showing of "Brave Heart" at the local theater. It was certainly a fitting place to view that film.

A wonderful day!

Mt. Snaeffels   3,036 ft.

Isle of Man.

October 27, 1995. Karla and I walked up the standard route to the top of the highest point on the Isle of Man. A class 2 hike, it is a gentle mountain, and it was a pleasant walk to the top. From the grassy ridge we could see Scotland, Ireland, and England. It was sunny but windy on top.

Mt. Washington   6,258 ft.

Presidential Range, New Hampshire.

August 26, 1995. Karla and I started from the Pinkham Notch, AMC Lodge area, and ascended the Tuckerman Ravine route and descended the Lion's Head route. This is the highest mountain in New England.

It was a fun climb, and a good accomplishment, as we had a day of rare good weather on a mountain that is noted for its rough weather. We visited the weather station located on the summit. There we saw some photos that showed how the summit looks in the winter time.

Mt. Whitney   14,494 ft.

Sierra Range, California.

November 25, 1995. Karla and I had great weather for our climb. Up at 3:00 a.m., we started at 4:15 a.m. from the trail head at Whitney Portal, at 8,360 feet. Throughout our climb, we saw only a two other people on the mountain.

The route we chose was class 2 and 3, and there were some shallow drifts of ice and snow on the last 1,000 feet to the summit. Elevation gained was a little over 6,000 feet. It was breezy and cold on top, but a good stone hut provided some shelter. We enjoyed the good views of the surrounding area.

We got back to the trail head and our T-100 pickup at 7:05 p.m..

It was a long, tough day. We were both very tired when we got back to our tent trailer at the camp ground near Lone Pine.

Mt. Angeles   6,554 ft.

Olympic Peninsula, Olympic National Park.

April 4, 1996. I ascended to the summit from the parking area on Hurricane Ridge and returned down the same route. It was a class 4 climb due to ice and snow in steep couloirs. Great views from the top. A short climb, but made somewhat difficult in places because of icy conditions near the summit.

Sheep Mountain   13,188 ft.

San Juan Mountains, Colorado.

June 24, 1996. Karla and me. Sheep Mt. is east of Lizard Head Pass, and there were lots of flowers, lots of elevation gain, and great views from the top. Another beautiful day, on another beautiful mountain.

Karla and I have changed the name of Lizard Head Pass to Moon Dog Pass.

Mt. Helmet   11,200 ft.

La Plata, Colorado.

June 8, 1996. A fine day on a Sierra Club climb. Our group consisted of 10 men and women, some from Durango and others from the Cortez area. We drove on a dirt road to a grassy parking spot up on the west slope of the mountain, which left us with a short distance to hike, and only a small elevation gain.

The going was easy, and there were good views of Cortez and Mesa Verde. There were lots of wild Iris in bloom in the meadow near where we left our vehicles.

Mt. Henkel   8,770ft.   Crowfeet Mt.   8,914 ft.

Many Glacier area, Glacier National Park.

July 27, 1996. Another beautiful day. A group of 9 of us met at the Swiftcurrent parking area and ascended Mt. Henkel. From there we went down a short distance to the saddle, then up again to the spectacular, narrow summit of Crowfeet. Iceberg Lake in the distance appeared to be still frozen over.

We descended to Ptarmigan Lake and then hiked back to Many Glacier by trail. The bear grass along the trail was in full bloom, and the white blossoms dotted the surrounding landscape.

Mt. Bachelor   9,065 ft

Oregon Cascades.

July, 1998. Karla and myself. We hiked the four miles of fairly steep but easy trail from the road to the summit. The hike up and back gave us a few hours of good exercise. We had good views of the surrounding central Oregon area from the summit.

On the way down, the trail goes through an area of lava rock. Karla was jogging for a ways, and she tripped on a lava rock on the trail, and fell into a pile of lava boulders. Some of them had very sharp edges, and she got a few cuts on the palms of her hands. Ouch!

Broken Top   9,175 ft.

Oregon Cascades.

August 24, 1998. After hiking into the Green Lakes area I climbed the northwest ridge route to the summit of Broken Top. It is a small, narrow summit, and there are interesting views of the surrounding countryside. On the descent via the same route, a rope would have been handy for a short pitch of class 4 just below the summit.

There were Indian Paintbrush and Asters in bloom along the lower part of the route. It took about 4 ½ hours to go from the trail head to the summit

Mt Thielsen   9,182 ft.

Oregon Cascades.

September 20, 1998. Karla and I spent the night in our tent at Diamond Lake CG. The next day, which was cool and sunny, we had breakfast at the Diamond Lake Lodge, and then we left the trail head at 8:00 a.m., and ascended Thielsen via the west ridge. There was about 4,000 feet of elevation gain, most of it by trail. Much of the route we used was an easy class 2, until the summit pitch, which was class 4. Karla, too pooped to go further, waited 100 yards from the summit.

There was a group of a dozen or so climbers on a Mazama

Club outing climbing the steep pitch below the summit. I had my rope with me, but they let me use their rope to rappel down from the small and narrow summit.

Goat Mt.   8,400 ft.

St. Mary Valley area, Glacier National Park.

July 27, 2001. A GMS group of 14 climbers that included Gordon Edwards, and led by Jane Edwards, took the trail from Sunrift Gorge up Baring Creek. When we reached a point below the summit we left the trail and climbed to the summit of the mountain.

It was about a 5 hour hike and 4,000 feet of elevation gain from the trail head. There were good views from the summit. Both the route up and the summit afford a different perspective of Going-to-the-Sun mountain than one is used to seeing from the road.

On our descent, Gordon showed us a great scree run which led from the summit ridge down to the trail below. We were back at the road and our vehicles by 6:00 p.m..

Haystack Butte   7,486 ft

Garden Wall area, Glacier National Park.

July 18, 2002. Our group of eight people started from the

Big Bend, Weeping Wall parking area and went up the creek bed to the Highline trail.

Before reaching the saddle, we left the trail and headed up to the top of Haystack Butte. The bear grass was in full bloom, and the views from the top were very nice. Haystack Butte towers above the Going-to-the-Sun Road, and is flanked on the north by the Highline Trail.

I think Haystack Butte is sometimes overlooked by climbers, perhaps because the surrounding peaks are much bigger, and its name suggests that it is, well, a butte. But it is indeed a worthwhile climb, and the views from the top are unique and spectacular.

After eating our lunch, and having a brief photo session, we descended the same route we went up. Nice weather, although somewhat cool and a bit windy. This was my first climb since undergoing cardiac bypass surgery, 4 ½ months earlier in March of 2002. It sure felt good to be back in the mountains again.

The Big Bend parking area where we left our vehicles was crowded with tourists, as is usual for this time of year. There is a huge avalanche that comes down here every spring, and covers the road. There is always a huge bank of snow above the road that is slow in melting away, and folks like to play on and around it. The park service places warning signs around it, but some folks pay no attention to them.

South Sister   10,358 ft.

Oregon Cascades.

September 10, 2002. A good celebration of Karla's 60th birthday! Ten of us, including some folks from St. Charles Hospital in Bend, started from the Devil's Lake campground. Barb, Laura, and Jenny from the cardiac rehab center at St. Charles led the climb. Our ascent route to the summit crater was via the south trail.

The round trip to the summit crater and back to Devil's Lake was a distance of 11 miles and there was an elevation gain of 4,900 feet.

Our route followed a trail all the way, but we climbed up some steep scree below the summit, which made for tough going. Great weather for our climb of this popular route. From the top we could see Bend, Redmond, Sisters, and the surrounding mountains, including Mt. Bachelor and of course the nearby Middle Sister and North Sister.

This was my second ascent of the South Sister. It's a good workout.

Mt. St. Helens   8,366 ft.

Washington Cascades

September 2, 2003. While on our way to Canada and Vancouver Island on our vacation, Karla and I camped at a

Summits and Trails

campground in the valley south of the mountain. The next day, which was nice, but smoky, we ascended the Monitor Ridge route to the summit ridge of St. Helens.

This is a popular route and climb. Several other groups were on the way up. The Forest Service has a permit system in effect for climbers during the busy season. We were fortunate to get a permit on short notice.

The route is mostly a trail of sorts, but it was tough going because of volcanic boulders, rocks and scree. We were 5 hours getting to the summit from the parking area, and there was an elevation gain of 4,600 feet. The view from the narrow rim of the summit ridge, above the huge crater, was impressive.

Visibility was a bit limited due to several forest fires in various locations in the distance. We were able to see the top of Mt. Adams, which we had climbed several years ago. After spending about a half hour on the crater rim, we descended by the same route, and in 4 hours were back to the trail head.

PART TWO

TRAILS

Trekking in Nepal

February 1, 1993.

Los Angeles Airport. As Karla drove our rental car through the suburbs of Los Angeles on our way to the airport, the radio reported several accidents and a sniper incident in areas of the city that we had just passed through.

After arriving at the terminal we boarded a beautiful Thai Airline plane, a relatively new plane with purple trim and decor. We have good seats, window and aisle, however we are at the break point between smoking and non-smoking sections, which is proving to be a bit of a nuisance. We have in-flight movies plus a choice of music via head-set. The crew is dressed in colorful Thai clothing, and I have just finished a complimentary Scotch on the rocks. The lunch menu has just been handed to us and it looks great.

This plane has rows of two seats on each side and five in the middle rows. We have side seats. It's a beautiful day with the blue Pacific below us. We are cruising at 31,000 feet and will go higher later. I think I am feeling the generous serving of excellent Scotch whiskey that the stewardess served. I'm feeling pretty mellow.

2:00 p.m. - just finished a gourmet lunch of chicken with almonds and rice, our choice of wine, chocolate cake and coffee are now being served. Karla is having tea with fresh lemon. Now, just as we thought we had seen everything in world class dining, we are now being served a liqueur. Wow! At this rate they will have to carry us off the plane! The music now playing is a waltz by Strauss. We have moved to seats further from the smoking area where we are far more comfortable.

February 2.

After landing at the airport in Tokyo we took a train to our Ryokan, then with the help of a policeman, caught a cab to the hotel.

We are pleased with the Ryokan. It is a traditional Japanese style hotel with bamboo mats on the floor. We are looking forward to seeing Akiko. We haven't seen her since she was a teenager. She was an exchange student who stayed with us at our home in Whitefish for two weeks a few years ago.

February 3.

Akiko's father, a very nice gentleman, met us this morning at the hotel and he took us on a tour of the city. He spoke very little English, but we enjoyed the tour. Poor Akiko is sick, but we had a great supper at her home and saw her for a while. Her two aunts and a friend who spoke some English were there also. After a short visit, we took our leave. It was a long day for us and we were glad to get back to the hotel at 9:30 p.m.

February 4.

This morning we walked to Uemo Park and visited the zoo. The Pandas were sleeping. Then we ate lunch at a small restaurant where they spoke no English. We enjoyed warm, sunny weather and strolled through business and residential areas.
At about 2:00 p.m., we took a train to Meguro to have supper with Nobuaki, Tomoko, Yashiko, Akiko, Tsutomu, and Akiko's boyfriend Taka. We had another special meal and gave the family their gifts. Akiko is feeling much better. We had fun, but the beer and Saki gave me a headache. After saying our goodbyes, Tsutomu drove us back to our Ryokan and we packed to be ready to get up and be on our way at 6:30 a.m.. We have to be at Narrita airport by 8:30, and our plane leaves at 10:30 a.m..

February 5.

At 6:15 we took a taxi to Uemo station and then took the train to the airport. Exchanged Yen for US dollars, and boarded our plane for Thailand. Just finished another excellent in-flight meal. The stewardess's dresses are very pretty.
We got a good look at snow covered Mt. Fuji above the clouds. The weather is sunny, the ocean is blue, and there are snow capped peaks on southern Japan island.
After arriving in Bangkok we caught a bus at the airport to downtown. Shanti Lodge was full, so we stayed at a place next door for 300 Bhat. Exchange rate in Thailand is about 25 to 1. Not good. Are we experiencing some culture shock? I think so.

February 6.

We slept well, and were up by 7:15 to plan the day. Mailed ten post cards, then took a water taxi to a shopping area. We had a good lunch where we first boarded the boat. It was a hot day, but the boat ride on the river was cool and enjoyable.
We each bought a couple of things. We cannot decide whether today is Friday or Saturday.
We checked out of the hotel this morning and now have a much better room at the Tavee Guest House, with a double bed and ceiling fan for 120 Bhat and we are much happier here. This guest house is a favorite with backpackers, and is reputed to be the best in this part of Bangkok.

February 7.

This morning we took a river taxi to Wat Arun, a temple where we spent an interesting few hours walking around and taking some photos. We had a good lunch at Shanti Lodge and afterwards had a two hour massage for 300 Bhat each. Tonight we are addressing more cards and plan to go to the palace tomorrow.

February 8.

Mailed more cards and then visited the palace. We were pretty much overwhelmed by the magnificence of that place; it is beautiful and it covers a large area. It was a bit crowded with tourists. We did manage to find a quiet and secluded place to sit in the shade. Then we went to Wat Po where we were blessed by a Buddhist monk and had water sprinkled on our heads and were given braided red, yellow and green string bracelets for good luck. He asked how the Chicago Cubs were doing.

Karla found a 10 Bhat note on the street on the way to our room, and with it we bought two strings of flowers to hang on the little Buddha shrine here at the guest house. The woman who manages the house says they will bring us good luck!

Phoned the airline and confirmed our flight to Kathmandu on the 10th. The weather was quite warm, but a breeze came up in the afternoon and cooled things off quite a bit and a shower at the house helped.

February 9.

Another hot day. We visited Vimanmek, a beautiful, quiet place and saw Thai dancers and museums. We also walked to Wat Benchamabophit and saw many statues of Buddhas. Had laundry done today and arranged for a mini bus to the airport in the morning at 7:30. Our flight for Nepal leaves at 11:55 a.m..

Temple in Kathmandu, Nepal.

February 10.

Kathmandu, Nepal. A few minutes after take-off our plane returned to Bangkok due to technical problems. We changed planes and arrived in Kathmandu two hours late. We were greeted outside the airport by a zillion taxi drivers. Namaste! We got a room at Holy Lodge for $14.00, or Rs. 700 a night. This city will be an experience for sure. Our room is on the top floor and very clean, brand new with a nice bath. We bought a map of the city and a trekking map of the Annapurna area.

February 11.

Walked to Durbar Square and to Swayambhunath. Had supper with Susan, a friend of Karla's, and with her Tibetan husband, Jam, at the Tibet Kitchen. They gave us some pointers on the area. I bought two souvenirs; a Mani stone and a prayer wheel for a total of Rs. 275. A great bargain even though my faulty hearing caused me to pay Rs.15 more for the prayer wheel than necessary. We are learning our way around Thamel and neighboring areas

February 12.

This morning we decided we have had enough of big city life for a while, and bought a tourist (mini) bus ticket to Pokhara for Saturday the 13th. It leaves at 7:00 a.m.. We left the return trip open. Then we took a 3 wheel to Bodinath and had a very enjoyable time at the stupa. There is a Tibetan settlement nearby and lots of Tibetans in the area. I bought a Buddha pendant and a bundle of prayer flags. This stupa is larger and more peaceful than Swayambunath. At the stupa area we were shown the Tibetan settlement temple with a large Buddha under construction. It will open in two months. Children in monk robes invited us in to look.

It was a sunny day, and we walked to the village of Arjivari searching for the Kimari family, but had no first name for them, so our search was fruitless. We were assisted by helpful Nepalese people, including a teacher at an English boarding school. The teacher's sister invited us to her house where we had a good visit, but we had to refuse tea because we were afraid of the water. A nice, quiet, small village, a farming community and beautiful people. Karla bought clothes on our return to Kathmandu. Tonight is clear with lots of stars out.

Restaurants we like in Kathmandu include KC's, Tibet's Kitchen, Mandap, Stupa View at Bodinath.

February 13.

The bus ride to Pokhara can be described in a few words; scary, with a few moments of horror interrupted by intervals of terror. During the six hour trip over winding roads and hills with steep drop offs on the lower side, we saw one dead body, three bus wrecks (bad) and two truck accidents (also bad). We do not wish to ride a Nepalese bus any more. The bus we were on was only Rs. 20 one way, but we think the drivers are crazy. At the bus stop in Pokhara we got a taxi to the Hotel Anzuk, a small, clean hotel where we have a room with bath for Rs. 300. There are lots of flowering plants on the balcony and around the hotel grounds.

Snake handler and Cobra - Kathmandu, Nepal.

Across the street there is what appears to be a bicycle rental shop. About a dozen bikes are lined up in a row in front of the shop, and at the far end of the row there is a water buffalo lying there taking a nap. That is an unusual sight, for us anyway.

We strolled around the neighborhood and are getting used to things. Karla has a sore throat, I hope it gets better soon.

February 14.

Spent the day walking around Pokhara. It is nice by the lake. We talked to some possible porters. The first asked $13.00 a day, the second $8.00. Some women here say it would be better to make arrangements through our hotel. Karla did some great bargaining on a necklace and beads and a spoon. She traded extra clothes.

We talked to a couple who had just finished the Annapurna circuit and sanctuary in three weeks. We have to talk to Vishnu, who is the clerk at our hotel, about a porter. The porter situation is confusing, we will be glad to have the matter settled. We are anxious to get on the trail.

February 15.

This morning we resolved to get this porter thing settled. We inquired at a couple of agencies, and were badgered by the two we met yesterday (one didn't show at Boomerang). We met with Vishnu at noon and hired Jiban, a young Hindu man in his twenties, for Rs. 400 a day. Of that, he buys his own food, etc. We went over the route on a map and Karla and I filled out trekking applications. Her cold is much better today. I have had stomach cramps, but nothing serious (I hope).

Tonight we plan to go to a Nepalese folk dance at Fishtail Lodge. We exchanged $300 at the bank to cover expenses for the trek. We will advance Jiban Rs. 2,000 to cover his expenses for the first five days of the trek. Normal porter costs vary from Rs. 375 to Rs. 600 and up. The captain (the hotel owner) gave us some tips on places to trek to if we feel up to it and/or have the time. This evening we attended the 1 hour cultural program at Fishtail Lodge which consisted of Nepalese music and dancing.

February 16.

When we got up this morning Karla laughed and said, "This ain't no Club Med! Oh, mommy, take me home". I agree. We joked that we could have spent our vacation in Watts or Harlem or the Bronx, but we are safer here, I hope. We are both feeling like we have had enough of cities, even though they have been interesting This is a nice hotel, and Pokhara is not that bad, but we are anxious to get out on the trail. I am into my second day of diarrhea with some stomach cramps, and on top of that a bird scored a direct hit just above my right shirt pocket.

We got our trekking permits today. The immigration office was not too bad, it took one hour of waiting this morning, then we returned at 3:00 p.m., to pick up permit. No problem. We are sorting out clothes for our trek, which we will start tomorrow morning at 9:00 and we learned that we won't need the foam pads.

We checked air fares from Pokhara to Kathmandu, then on to Lukla and a return to Kathmandu. No more busses for us! The airline people want their pay in US dollars.

A sign in the lobby of our Hotel Anzuk reads "THE MANAGEMENT DOES NOT TAKE RESPONSIBILITY IF YOU ARE OVERCHARGED OR CHEATED BY ANYONE OTHER THAN CAPTAIN GURUNG THE OWNER - EX BRITISH GURKHA."

Oh well, translating from one language to another can sometimes prove to be a bit embarrassing. We know what the captain meant.

February 17.

On the trail at last! Now we can see why trekking is such a great thing to do! We are really enjoying this. Jiban, our porter is carrying our sleeping bags and a few clothes and we each have our day packs with personal gear. After our first 2 ½ hours on the trail we are having a lunch of vegetable soup and tea at the Dhaulagiri Hotel in Dhampus. Jiban, our porter, had daal bhaat for lunch. It looks really good. It is a plate of rice and lentils, and sometimes served with a fresh vegetable. It is a very popular dish here in Nepal. We will probably try it for supper. We are up quite high above the valley and have caught glimpses of the mountains through the clouds. Beautiful, clean countryside, nice weather, some prayer flags here and there, all the trail so far is paved with stone, but steep.

We started our trek at Suikhet and have a room at an inn in Potham for Rs.10 per person. We took turns with other trekkers playing guitar and singing in the evening.

We really appreciate the quiet beauty of the area we are passing through.

February 18.

After tea and chapatis with honey and jam this morning, Karla took a Polaroid photo of the family. It turned out great, so we were immediately asked to take photos of the others, which she did. It was fun to do and we gave them the photos.

We started our trek at 8:30 this morning and Fishtail and Annapurna South were very much in view. It had rained during the night and the mountains were very visible. It is now noon and we are at an inn and school in Tolka, waiting for potatoes to boil while carpenters and stone masons are working on a small, new house next door. They are making lap-joint flooring with small adzes. We have a delicious lunch of boiled potatoes, cooked greens and yak cheese and tea. The day, like all of them so far, is sunny. Temperature is about seventy degrees.

We are spending the night at a small village called Landrung. It rained briefly this evening, but now the sun is out again. We are not too impressed by this inn but we will try the food. We are the only ones here. The owner speaks pretty good English. He says Chomrong, where we go tomorrow, is mostly Buddhist. Jiban went to spend the night with a relative not far from here.

February 19.

South Annapurna was very clear when we got up this morning. We had tea and chapatis and started walking at 8:15 a.m.. We followed the river Modi Khola and are now stopped for lunch at Kyumrung. Jiban is having daal bhaat again, the traditional, cultural, Nepalese dish. Karla and I are having corn bread with boiled potatoes and a bowl of vegetables on the side and black tea.

Chomrong, where we will spend the night, is about 1 ½ hours from here. We talked to some trekkers who are returning from Annapurna Base Camp and they say the days are warm but it gets very cold at night. We have done a lot of climbing so far today. The rain only lasted for a short time this afternoon and we were sweating on the climb up to Chomrong.

We arrived at Chomrong, a beautiful village with a great view of the mountain, Machhapuchhre (Fishtail) and are staying at the Chomrong Guest House. The guest houses and lodges along the trail are usually small, stone buildings with a kitchen, dining area, and a few small bedrooms with cots or bunks in them. Once in a great while, however, a village that is on a much traveled trail will have a lodge that is 2 or 3 stories high.

After a hot shower we had garlic soup, vegetable omelet and Tibetan bread for supper. We will put our beds together tonight for warmth.

February 20.

We walked 8 hours from Chomrong to the Himalaya Lodge, which is at about 2,800 meters. The trail was on the west side, up from the river bottom, and mostly uphill as we entered a large canyon. Now we are sitting at a table with a kerosene heater under it, watching it snow outside. There are a Swiss couple, a Japanese couple, a couple from Germany, and Jiban. We have all ordered supper and are waiting for the food to be served. Another American has just joined us, a man from San Francisco. He looks more like he could be a Hasidic Jew from Israel. Now there is also a man from India. A very interesting international group.

Jiban is always seated last, although sometimes he orders first. We asked him about this and he says it is just the custom, as he is only a porter.

I have to say that we are very pleased with our choice of Jiban as our porter. He is a helpful and efficient travel companion, and has a working knowledge of several languages.

For supper we had tea, fried potatoes, vegetable soup, chapatis and fried noodles, which were like spaghetti with cheese on top. It was still snowing, big flakes. Everyone was discussing McDonald restaurants and Kentucky Fried Chicken.

It has finally stopped snowing and the sky is clearing up. It's 8:00 p.m., and we haven't been up this late in days. At the suggestion of the man from Japan, we all took turns singing national songs. I sang "Country Roads" and was surprised that most of them knew the English words to the song. The Japanese man has a great sense of humor, but speaks very little English.

All of us are looking forward to making it to base camp.

A snow covered route below Annapurna Base Camp - Nepal.

February 21.

Annapurna Base Camp, 4,000 meters, 4:30 p.m.. This pen is frozen, so now I am using a pencil to write in this journal. It was snowing and the temperature was 10 above zero as we were on our way here from Machhapuchhre Base Camp. Snow is about six inches deep here, and it is very cold. Karla's hair is frozen.

The trail was tricky coming up here, narrow and slippery. I gave Jiban a dry pair of wool socks, as his were thin and wet. All he has are worn tennis shoes with holes in them, and the soles are very smooth. He wrapped plastic bags around them to help keep his feet dry.

We crossed the river on an interesting footbridge today, which proved to be stronger then it appeared. We heard and saw lots of icefall avalanches as we traveled along the trail. It will be very dangerous going down from here, as the trail is steep and icy. I think it will take a long time.

We are sitting around a long wooden table with the Swiss couple and a woman and two men from Israel who were in Tel Aviv when the SCUD missiles were coming in. It's really interesting to talk to them.

It is dark in here and hard to write. We have ordered fried potatoes and fried noodles. This lodge is far nicer than I expected, but the higher we climb the more expensive the food becomes.

The food is very good. It is amazing the quality and kinds of food these people can cook with such limited facilities. It is delicious and there is always plenty of it. There is one Nepalese man cooking for us, plus pumping up the stoves, carrying water, etc.. He is very busy all the time.

It's an incredible feeling to be here at the Annapurna

Base Camp. Now we have a gas lantern going.

The Swiss couple have been traveling for 16 months, and the folks from Israel have been to China and Tibet. We are having quite a discussion about Japanese vs. U.S. vs. European automobiles.

There are two kerosene heaters under the table, and blankets are hanging around the table so we put the blankets over our laps and feel the heat, but we can still see our breath. It is now 7:30 p.m.. We have eaten our potatoes and are waiting for fried noodles, and we are already full.

Our plan originally was to spend a day here, but now because of the weather we will probably start down about 10:00 a.m., and see how far we will get.

February 22.

When we awoke this morning it was clear and beautiful, but very cold. We both felt the altitude a little during the night and had headaches, but we were OK when we got up. We took lots of photos, including one of the cook and one with the Polaroid of Jiban next to the Annapurna Base Camp sign, which he had requested that we do.

We started back down at 9:00 a.m., and by 11:00 we were in heavy snow which made the trail even more treacherous. We walked until 3:30 and decided to spend the night at Dovandi.

There are just Karla and I and 6 Nepalese, including our porter. I am writing this by candlelight. The stove under the table is very warm, and we are drying clothes on our laps.

Jiban had a tough time today. He fell many times on the slippery trail.

This is our sixth day trekking. Tomorrow should be a

short day to Chomrong, but it will still be slow going because of wet trails. For supper we are having vegetable fried rice with Tibetan bread. For lunch we had vegetable noodle soup.

I think we were lucky to have had six inches of snow at base camp as it made the surroundings very beautiful. Even Jiban said he had never seen it so beautiful. We think the weather has turned many trekkers back. It would be very difficult to get up there now. Our timing was very good.

The fumes from the kerosene stove/heater are starting to get to us. There are now nine Nepalese here and a couple small bottles of wine have appeared.

February 23.

Back at Chomrong. It's a lot warmer here, and a warm shower felt good. We left Dovandi at 9:00 a.m., and got here at 6:30 p.m.. We slept really well last night - went to bed at 6:30 p.m., and got up at 7:30 the next morning.

It took us a long time to get down out of the snow this morning. The Bamboo forest was flocked with snow and the snow fell on us from the leaves and branches as we got lower.

Walking sticks of bamboo work really well. At the check point here in Chomrong the man told Karla, "Don't miss it, it is a good friend!"

At our lunch stop Karla took some Polaroids of some children. They were a lot of fun. Some chickens were in a cage in the background in the photo with one of the little boys, and he took the photo over to their cage and showed it to them. One of the little girls painted Karla's fingernails red, and I let her do one of mine. She also put a red dot on Karla's forehead. We had a great lunch of vegetable noodle soup and Tibetan bread.

Lower down we walked past Rhododendron trees that were starting to bloom. On the trail there was one group of children that I gave photos of the Dalai Lama to. They wanted all the photos, so now I have only one left on a postcard. Jiban says that most of the people north of Chomrong are Buddhist, while most of the people where we will be going next are Hindu.

Tonight we will have fried potatoes and eggs. I had rice pudding for breakfast, and it was really good. It is now 6:30 p.m., and it has been raining for at least an hour. The Japanese couple just got here. We are waiting for them to come to the table so we can hear about their day. As usual, there are several languages being spoken at once around the table, but most people speak English as a second language.

February 24.

Chulkli, Hill Side Lodge, lunch time. More Tibetan bread, noodle soup, tea, and macaroni with tomato. We left Chomrong at 8:20 a.m., and on our way here we saw a band of monkeys and were very close to several vultures. There are a few Rhododendron in bloom, but not many. Karla has had more fun with the Polaroid taking several photos of children and mothers,. It is getting cooler as we climb, and feels like it might rain again. We hope to reach Tarapan before it starts. It is about 1 ½ hours further.

It is now 2:50 p.m., and we have made it to Tarapan where we will spend the night. We did a lot of climbing to get this far. We had a close look at a group of white monkeys on the way up. It is about 8,000 feet here and quite cool.

We are in a nice lodge, and there is a wood stove in the "dinning" room. The view from here is supposed to be good, but it is clouded in at the moment. This is our eighth day trekking.

We have met a woman from Australia who is an expedition group director/leader and taking a day off. Very interesting and well traveled. We discussed "Tracks" by Robyn Davison. A man is telling us about the Khumbu region. He went from Lukla to Tengboche and said it was not difficult walking, even at that altitude.

There were many tall Lali Guras, or Rhododendron trees, in the forest on the way up, and a kind of white flower on bushes three or four feet high that smelled strongly of perfume and made the whole forest smell sweet. There was also lots of moss on the trees.

Karla did her laundry of several sets of undies, or "Montana Prayer Flags." There are 16 of us around this wood stove, and about four different languages being spoken at once. There are several tents set up outside, and many of the group are in here. They are not headed for base camp. However, we met two English women from Yorkshire, probably in their fifties, on the trail this morning who were headed that way. They appeared to be a bit out of shape, and I have to wonder if they'll make it or not.

More fried potatoes with cheese and tomato soup for supper tonight. The Tibetan bread we had for lunch was made from corn, and had a completely different look and taste than the Tibetan bread we were used to.

We have not yet decided whether or not to go to Lukla and the Everest region after we get back from this trek.

February 25.

It has been a long, hard climb from Tarapan to where we have just stopped for lunch and now we are just under 10,000 feet. The day is cloudy, and there is a bit of snow on the ground. Karla is having a time trying to keep warm and dry when we stop. I talked her into putting on my wool sweater. I think the hard climbing is over now, and it is not far to Ghorepani.

We arrived at Ghorepani at 9,250 feet at 2:45 this afternoon. We are staying at Pun (Poon) Hill Lodge, which had been recommended to us. The sun came out sporadically and after we got our room it rained briefly.

Karla said, "Let's take a look around the bend," so we ended up climbing Pun Hill before supper. Elevation of Pun Hill is 10,478 feet. Due to high clouds the view was somewhat restricted, but still the climb up there was well worth the effort.

We got back to our lodge at 5:03 p.m., and ordered daal bhaat, fried rice, and Tibetan bread with yak cheese. We are sitting close to the fire after a good supper. Jiban is giving Nepalese language lessons to an older Japanese man. The porters are eating their daal bhaat. It is nice and warm in here. Tomorrow we go to Tatopani, on the Kali Gandaki river. It should be almost all downhill, but probably a 7 hour trip anyway.

We are still discussing whether or not to go to the Everest region.

February 26.

It is 12:00 noon, and we are eating lunch at Ghara, on the way to Tatopani. We spent a good night at Pun Hill Lodge, and were on the trail at 7:50 a.m.. On the way here we met several pack trains with burros carrying supplies. Each animal was decorated with brightly colored wool and tassles. We also saw another group of white monkeys.

As we go lower, there are many 20 or 30 feet high Rhody trees in full bloom. We pass through many small villages and by some schools. Now we are using the Polaroid again, taking photos of a family that lives in a dwelling beside the trail, and have two small children. They changed into their best clothes for the occasion. Jiban is taking the photos.

After the third or fourth pack train had passed, one of the packers showed us a deep, fresh puncture wound in his forearm, and asked if we had any medicine. We got out our first aid kit and put some antibiotic salve and a bandage on his wound. The salve contained a pain reliever. We told him, through Jiban, to seek medical help in Ghorepani.

It took seven hours to get to Tatopani, all down hill. We got our room and headed for the hot springs at Kamala Lodge. The springs were hot alright and there were ten or twelve people there. It was a communal bath, and it felt good to wash in hot water. We are having the hotel do some laundry for us too.

We are down out of the high country, and this town has shops that sell various items that are not found in the mountain villages higher up. Also, for the first time since Pokhara, there are people selling jewelry, etc. There are orange and lemon trees here with fresh fruit on them.

February 27.

Our eleventh day on the trail. We slept until 8:00 a.m., and then had a Tibetan breakfast. The lodge man brought complimentary fresh oranges to our table. Karla found a beautiful piece of material for a Nepal style dress. I am having a Tibetan woman make a woven bracelet of colors I chose. She invited us to her shop for tea with yak butter at three this afternoon. The woman says that she is waiting to return to Tibet when it is free. She says there are no jobs here for Tibetans, but she is lucky and has a shop.

It is nice to have a day to just loaf around. There have been several pack strings go through. This village on the Kali Gandaki is on an old trade route between Tibet and India. It is a small village (but there is a bank here) with one narrow street, a few shops and lodges. All caravans pass right through town.

Karla made a deal for some socks, a cap and a dress by trading a tee shirt and a Polaroid photo with the Tibetan woman. We spent the afternoon just sitting on the steps along the street watching the people pass by. The weather was sunny until about 3:00 and then by 5:00 it had become a bit cool. We had our laundry done, it was washed on the rocks below the hot springs. Karla had an orange drink and I had more black tea.

A short while ago a German trekker came in who we had met at Annapurna Base Camp, and whose knee bothered him going down hill. He told us that he had talked to people who said the trail to Annapurna base camp is closed from the Himalaya Hotel onwards because of deep snow and avalanches. We feel very lucky to have reached base camp when we did. He said he was told that an avalanche came in the window of a lodge at Gurung. I think that was where the Belgium couple spent the night on their way out. We wondered how the other trekkers that we had met at base camp fared on their way down from there.

We have decided to do some trekking in the Solu Khumbu, Mt Everest region. We will try to fly into Lukla and trek to Namche Bazaar and then on to the Tengboche monastery. We will talk with Royal Nepal Airlines when we get back to Kathmandu. We have ordered supper to be served at 6:30. Karla is having spaghetti and I asked for daal bhaat. For desert we are having apple crumble. It is raining, a brief mountain shower, and we are sitting at a table under a roof, out of the wind, where we can watch people, and drinking our lemon tea.

Some of the sounds that we hear are greetings of Namaste, children chattering and at play, the deep ringing of loud bells on pack animals, the river as it rushes through the boulders, Nepali and sometimes American songs on the hotel radio. Now we hear the wind whooshing through the buildings and the orange and lemon trees, the sound of pots banging in the kitchen as supper is being cooked, conversations in several languages as trekkers gather for supper. There is usually the sound of a flute somewhere in most villages we pass through. Namaste.

February 28.

Day 12. This has been a long hard day from Tatopani to Beni. We started at 8:00 a.m., and arrived here at 4:00 p.m., one of the longer days on the trail that we have had and we are both feeling it, although it was all downhill except when we had to go high to get by sheer rock cliffs. We followed the Kali Gandaki, which runs through one of the world's deepest gorge through the Himalaya, all the way to Beni. Nilgiri was covered with fresh snow and then what appeared to be South Annapurna became dominant as we looked back up the gorge.

We used the Polaroid just once, at a place along the trail where there was a small girl holding a baby goat. It would have made a great shot for the 35mm but we were too tired to even think of it. The photos we have taken should make a really great slide show and I am looking forward to putting one together. I do not like to think that tomorrow is the last day of this trek. The days have flowed together naturally and quietly and I do not want the routine broken by our return to the cities.

There are boys watering plants in the garden where our dining table is located. There is a sunflower and lots of red flowers that I don't know the names of.

It was sunny most of the day, but in the early afternoon it clouded up and a cool breeze came up the river. A short distance before Beni we came to a concrete structure with a small head of a buffalo cast in brass, with cold spring water spewing out of its mouth, and it felt really refreshing to splash some of the cold water on our faces and hands.

Jiban says that during the rainy season the Kali Gandaki becomes a raging torrent. I think this river is one of the headwaters of the Ganges. I'll have to look at a map and see. The plan for tomorrow is to walk to Baglung and catch a truck in the afternoon to Pokhara. For the first time on the trek Karla's feet are tired and sore. She has no blisters though, and we are both glad of that,. My feet are tired also. I would like to know how many kilometers we walked today, but our map does not show scale, and Nepalis measure distance by hours and minutes between points.

Chickens are common to see in almost every village, so eggs are plentiful At this point we have passed through over thirty villages that are shown on our map, and I know there were many smaller ones that were not shown. I would have to refer to the guide book to name the different ethnic groups that inhabited the areas we passed through, but Jiban tells us that it is the Gurung who inhabit the country up the Modi Khola leading to the Annapurna Sanctuary. Many of them have served in the Gurkha regiments.

We just took a very short stroll down the street in Beni. There are lots of children playing games, and donkeys turned loose to rest and water with their packs off for the night. The buildings on each side of the street seem very old, with the usual carved wooden doors and wooden trim.

March 1.

It is a four hour walk to Baglung, which is sort of a boom town. They are blasting the hillside and building the road on up the gorge. The hills now get smaller and the bottom land widens to allow farming. There must have been at least 200 donkeys on the trail, carrying loads of rice and flour north.

We got to Baglung at noon, just in time to climb into the open back of a Chinese made truck that soon became packed with people. The first two hours on the road were very dusty and dirty. We had no lunch, and we arrived in Pokhara at 4:00 p.m.. We had a hot shower at Hotel Anzuk. The Captain praised us for making it to base camp. We have a large, nice common room for Rs. 120. The mountains are clearly visible north of the city.

We celebrated our return by eating at Fishtail Lodge, It was a really good buffet, although a bit expensive for Nepal. We felt guilty eating the fancy food.

We paid Jiban his wages that were due, plus an Rs.1000 tip and some clothing. We were sorry to have to say goodby. He had been a very good porter. Now, at 9:30 p.m., we are off to bed.

March 2.

There is not a cloud in the sky this morning. We are having breakfast of toast, eggs and tea on the roof of the Anzuk. The mountains are beautiful. We have to get organized today for our flight to Kathmandu tomorrow. We read in the papers that Princess Diana is in Kathmandu and the King and Queen of Nepal were in Pokhara yesterday.

We walked uptown and got our plane tickets to

Kathmandu and then bought a couple of folk music tapes. We notice that in Tibetan shops there are always photos of the Dalai Lama. We skipped lunch because we had a huge breakfast. The weather has been sunny all day although now the mountains are hidden in clouds We know they are there, however!

Our Everest Airline plane leaves at 9:55 tomorrow morning for Kathmandu. Karla contacted the Nepal View hotel and we have reserved a room and will be met at the airport. Once there, we will have to start arranging for a visa extension and our trekking permits for Solu Khumbu. Now we are catching glimpses of the snow covered mountains once more as we have our little "happy hour" on the rooftop of our hotel. We appreciate the beauty of this town so much more now that we have returned and the visibility has improved.

We are chatting with a young couple who have just arrived from Chitwan and hope to trek to Annapurna base camp, and we are enjoying the relaxed traveling lifestyle.

March 3.

It's a clear day allowing great views. We are on our 14 passenger (plus a stewardess) Everest Airline plane, a Dornier twin engine STOL (Short Takeoff or Landing) aircraft, cruising at 10,000 feet. We have seats on the mountain side, and are passing Manaslu on our way to Kathmandu, which will be a thirty minute flight.

On arrival we are met and taken to our room in the Nepal View Hotel. We like this hotel. It has a friendly, efficient staff, and we have a nice, airy room with a bath, double bed and phone for $10.00 U.S..

We had a light lunch and then went to Nepali airlines and bought two round trip tickets to Lukla. The flight is to leave at 8:00 a.m., March 5, and return on the 15th which is a few days early to insure a good chance of flight connections, as weather affects Lukla flights greatly.

There was a man who introduced himself as Ang Temba Sherpa and his wife at the office also, buying tickets, and he was helpful in telling us about hiring a porter and getting a hotel in Lukla. Maybe we can avoid the crowds of would-be porters at the airport. We might hire a Sherpina to carry our duffel. We tried immigration this afternoon at 2:30 but they were closed, so we will have to go there in the morning to get our permits and visa extensions.

We walked to Pilgrims Books and got some Nepalese stationary and more cards, plus a poster of the Annapurna Range and photos of the Dalai lama. We also stocked up on small wooden boxes of tea for gifts. This city does not seem so overwhelming as it did when we first arrived three weeks ago. I guess we are over our first exposure and are accepting it for what it is, even after two weeks of relative solitude while trekking.

We had quite an experience for supper. We went to the Yak and Yeti, a classy hotel with two dining areas plus a large coffee shop. We ate in the theater dining room where there were crystal chandeliers, a stage, white tablecloths and white-gloved waiters, and watched an hour of a folk dance troupe performing while we ate. The food was very good. The building was built as a theater-palace in 1855 and is very elegant, with marble imported from Italy.

March 4.

Today was a four hour ordeal waiting in line at immigration getting our permits for the Solu Khumbu in the Everest region. With that finally done we returned to the hotel, packed our trekking gear, put one duffle in storage and made preparations for an early flight to Lukla at 7:00 a.m. tomorrow. We also made reservations at the hotel for the eve of our return to Kathmandu on March 15.

For lunch at the hotel we had "Cobra Eyes," a very good dish with round meat patties, sauce, fried rice, salad, and mashed potatoes with cheese. This dish tastes very good, much better than the name implies.

After lunch we went to the district of Thamel and walked around. The streets of the Thamel area are narrow and crowded, with merchants and roadside vendors trying to get you to buy. We are kept busy dodging traffic of all sorts; rickshaws, taxis, people, all going very fast and missing each other and everything by scant inches. It's like a midway at a county fair.

Tonight we are eating at a Thai restaurant. There is a slide show on rafting and kayaking in Nepal which we watched while eating. Karly is still writing postcards. The card selection in the shop where she purchased the cards is incredible.

March 5.

Up this morning at 5:30, we weren't able to flag down a taxi until 6:30 but still made it to the airport on time, where Ang Temba Sherpa met us and helped get us on the plane, a STOL which seats 12 passengers, plus the stewardess.

We had a great view of the mountains on our flight to Lukla, where there is a rather short, steep and uphill dirt and rock landing strip. I understand that Hillary was instrumental in the building of the airfield. On the lower end of the strip there is a steep cliff.

Heeding Temba's advice, we went to the K2 Lodge,

owned by a relative of Temba's, Nima, who, judging by the photos on the wall, sumitted on K2 in 1989 with a tri-country expedition that included Chinese and Japanese climbers.

Sherpa country is really different from the Pokhara area. Temba, who has been to 8,400 meters with a Dutch team on Pumo Ri, was very helpful. He fixed us up with a Sherpina whose name is Kanjee, at Rs. 300 a day. She will buy her own food and lodging. We offered to pay Temba for the help he had given us, but he refused to take money or some kind of tip. He said he did it all as a friend. Karly took Polaroids of Temba and his wife and kids and gave them the photos. That made quite a hit.

When Kanjee arrived at the lodge, we started on our trek. We walked for three hours, including a tea stop, to the village of Phakding, On the way, the trail passed by Kanjee's home, and she invited us inside her small, stone, home with a fireplace for warmth and cooking, where she made tea and introduced her children. They will stay with relatives while she is away. Her husband had been out on a trek too, and after hiking a short distance, we met him on the trail. He and Kanjee spoke briefly, then we continued on our separate ways.

We followed the Dudh Khosi and there were lots of Mani Stones and prayer flags along the trail. Our porter always takes care to pass those places on the left. After a while, I do too, as I am thinking maybe Buddhism is a good philosophy, so I will try to do as they do to experience it more.

After we arrived at Phakding, a small village at an altitude of 2,600 meters, we had some Yak cheese and got a room for the night at Rs. 60. Kanjee went back to her home for her coat. Looks like tomorrow we will go to Namche Bazaar, at 11,234 feet, a four hour walk where we should spend a day to acclimatize.

Summits and Trails

We left our airplane return tickets to Kathmandu with the people at the K2 Lodge, along with the clothes for our porter that will serve as a "tip" when we return. We feel very comfortable doing this.

The wind came up this afternoon, and when the sun goes down it will be quite cool, I think. We are here at the start of the trekking season, before the crowds arrive. We get the impression that some of the inns are just opening up. This is a good time to trek.

March 6.

Day two of our Solu Khumbu trek. I am writing this in the Thewa Lodge where we are staying in Namche Bazaar. This is a pretty incredible town site, with houses built on steep hillsides. The weekly Saturday market is over, but some Tibetans are still here selling things. It took us six hours to get here from Phakding. The last two hours was a steep climb and we are both tired. We had a brief view of Ama Dablam, and in the morning we will climb to a hill above town where it is said we will see Mt. Everest.

March 7.

Gary has a combination of a cold and altitude sickness, and asked me to bring the journal up to date. He had a horrible night, not sleeping from about 11:00 p.m. on. About 8:30 a.m., we walked up to the ridge. Gary had a tough time but he made it. We had fabulous views of Ama Dablam, Lhotse and Everest. We visited the museum on the ridge that had interesting pictures of local flora, fauna and a history of Mt. Everest climbs.

After returning to the lodge, Gary slept until about

1:00 p.m.. He could only eat a couple of bites of Ra Ra soup for lunch. He thinks he will be well enough to continue tomorrow, we shall see. Kanjee must speak a different dialect of Sherpa language as she does not understand words I point to in our English/Sherpa dictionary. Perhaps she cannot read.

She wanted two days pay, so we gave her Rs. 600. She bought something for her dress, we think. Her dress is a wool, bib apron type garment that she wears over a full length gray gown.

March 8.

Started trekking on the trail along the Dudh Kosi and arrived at Tengboche, a very small village situated at 12,606 feet. We took it really easy coming up here, and I hope it will make a difference. I am surprised that I have had a problem with altitude. I felt much better this morning. Karla has really adapted well to the altitude.

We were six hours getting here from Namche, and the last 3 hours was steep uphill all the way. We saw a deer resting just off the trail as we were coming up the steepest part. On reaching the village we walked through a Buddhist entryway.

Karla got here first and got us a room at Tengboche Guest House for Rs. 50. It looks like we will be the only ones here, I hope. The other guest houses are full except for the dormitories. The views should be great in the morning. I shaved and washed in our room. Karly brought basins of hot water, but it was cool when we used it. After getting settled in our room, we toured the new monastery here that replaces the old one that was destroyed by fire in 1989.

Kanjee has a headache. We hope she is better by morning.

Lhotse and Mt. Everest from the Tengboche Monastery - Nepal.

Kanjee, our Sherpina porter.

The woman who runs this lodge speaks pretty good English. She lives in Namche Bazaar but comes up here during trekking season. She has the Sherpa Lodge "upside"in Namche. She is 48, and has four daughters and one boy. She said that last night six Koreans with porters stayed here on their way to climb Everest. They were packing their gear on yaks. She also said that Sir Edmund Hillary usually stays at least four nights at her lodge in Namche every year in April or May. He arrives by helicopter and visits the Hillary hospital and school. Sometimes Peter comes with him.

March 9.

After taking the right-hand fork of the trail at the place where the Khumbu and Imja Kola meet, we arrived here in Dingboche at about 14,450 feet at 2:15 p.m., after a five hour walk. The left-hand fork would have taken us to Pheriche, which we plan to visit from our base at Dingboche.

It is cold up here. Kanjee felt better as the day wore on. She was humming little tunes for the last few hours. Karla is still taking the altitude really well while I am still feeling not quite up to par. She goes ahead and gets the lodging lined up.

We are staying at the Sonam Friendship Lodge. We are in a dormitory with several other trekkers. Tomorrow will be a rest day, then on the 11th we will start back down.

Apparently, an American couple were married here last night in a ceremony complete with chang, which is a kind of beer, Sherpa songs, white scarves, and butter in their hair.

The Sherpa that owns this lodge speaks pretty good

English, and has been telling us about what happened to Tenzing Norgay, the Sherpa who accompanied Hillary on his Mt. Everest climb in 1953. We hear that there were riots in Kathmandu three of four days ago.

It is interesting that in the lodge there is a photo of Jimmy and Rosalynn Carter that was taken in front of the Khumbu Lodge in Namche. Also hanging on the wall is a Xmas card photo of Diane Feinstein and her husband. Sonam said that she trekked to Island Peak in 1985 (?) with the intention of climbing it, but the weather turned bad.

March 10.

The food is great here. The daal bhaat looks really good. We went for a day hike of about 4 ½ hours, up on the ridge west of the village. We must have gained 1,500 feet and we had spectacular views. I'm sure we saw Cho-oyu. We should have some good photos.

We came upon an assortment of stone buildings and caves, way up high on the steep slopes of the mountain above the village. There were lots of Buddhist things, such as mani stones and prayer flags. It was a wonderful place to explore. We saw smoke coming from one of the dwellings and made our way to it and shouted, "namaste." In a short while an old woman appeared, prayer wheel in hand, and chanting "om mani padme hum" over and over. We gave her some biscuits, a couple of pencils and a nylon scarf. Unfortunately, I had left all my photos of the Dalai Lama at the lodge.

Mani Stones by a trail in Nepal.

Monastery at Tengboche.

Typical foot bridge across a river in Nepal.

Pack animals on a trail in Nepal.

A stone cairn and Yak horns with carvings on them.

Karla and Nepalese children having fun with the Polaroid camera.

Gary and Karla high on the slopes above Dengboche, with Ama Dablam in the background.

By her gestures we think that she invited us to tea, but we declined. Pointing with our hands, we asked her what was the way down, and she pointed the way with gnarled, twisted fingers. We asked if we could take her picture and she saw our camera and nodded "yes." Then she started walking around and around a small pile of Mani stones, and I took a photo as she paused briefly. As we made our way down the steep hillside, we looked back and saw her standing on the point by a prayer flag, waving at us. We waved back several times. It was a memorable experience.

We told the lodge owner about her, and he knew her. He said that the area up there on the steep mountain side has been used for meditation since the 10th century. Karla was told by the owner that the woman had been up there for two years. The Nangkartshang Gompa, or temple, at 15,430 feet was the highest point of our trek.

It is now 2:10 p.m., and we have had bowls of Sherpa stew and chipatis with the usual black tea. It is getting colder outside, and the wind chill made it cold this morning too. We heard that there is a lecture on altitude sickness just over the ridge at Pheriche at three o'clock, so we might decide to hike over there.

A few more trekkers have arrived at the lodge. We keep meeting the same people over and over. Going down tomorrow there should be bright new faces coming up!

We decided to walk over to Pheriche. It only took twenty minutes to get there, and the lecture by an English woman who is a doctor, and an Australian man who is also a doctor, was well worth the walk. They told about the physiology of mountain sickness and explained how Diomox works. If one does not feel well when at altitude, it should be treated as altitude sickness until proven otherwise. We saw their pressure chamber, and their little office seemed well stocked with medicine. We came back in a pleasant snow storm, just enough to make the ground white. Now, at 5:15 p.m., it has stopped snowing and there is lots of blue sky showing.

Makalu was in view from the ridge this morning. There is a cassette player in the lodge. It is in the kitchen and there are speakers in the dining and sleeping area. It is playing a classical tape of beautiful music.

There is an older couple from Minnesota here among the guests. They are school teachers at the university, he in human services, and she has a masters in psychology. They are on sabbatical. They spent a year in Africa and also were in South America. She could be a twin of a friend of ours back in Washington. About the same age and has the same looks. They showed us photos of their cabin in the Boundary Waters area of Minnesota. This lodge has been a wonderful experience. Good group, management, food, and a warm stove that they burn yak chips in.

March 11.

We left Dingboche at 8:30 a.m., and in less then 4 hours arrived Tengboche at 12:15. It was all downhill except for the last short section. Before we left this morning, we asked the owner if he would let us take a photo of our duffel being loaded on a yak, which he did. The ground was white with a light covering of snow, but we soon had to stop and take off some clothes. We passed a group of Sherpina porters headed for Everest base camp loaded with pink boxes of supplies for the Korean Everest expedition.

Old woman near her hut high on the slopes above Dengboche.

So here we are, starting on the return leg of our journey. We have our old room at the lodge. At this point we are the only ones here, but that could change as it is early and more trekkers might arrive heading either up or down. We have ordered our lunch of Sherpa stew, french fries, chipatis and black tea.

We are, of course, still in Sagarmatha National Park, and will not leave it until we go from Namche to Phakding. Again, we are reminded that we are here at a very good time, ahead of the crowds.

A Sherpa tells us that soon the area below the monastery and between the lodges will be covered with tents for about two months before the rains come. Then he will close his lodge and take his yaks to the high country to graze until September, then will return and re-open his lodge. Also in September is scheduled the opening of the new monastery. The huge Buddha and figures inside were made by a group of workers from Bhutan. He says the whole project was very expensive.

It is now 3:30 p.m.. A yak outfit has just pulled in from Kali Pattar, with another group of Germans. They said they left camp at 3:30 a.m.. Their tents are being set up, but they all came in here to the dormitory as it is cold and snowing outside. So much for having the place to ourselves. We are glad that we have a private room.

March 12.

Friday, 2:00 p.m., Chomkang Trekker's Lodge in Namche Bazaar. Interesting day.

We have the room that Hillary uses when he visits here each spring. How this came about is as follows.

Karla took Polaroid photos of the woman who owns the lodge in Tengboche, and also of her daughter. The woman wrote a note for us to give to her other daughter at her lodge in Namche, which we delivered along with the photos. We got a half rate on the room. The daughter has two babies, speaks pretty good English, and has a degree in hotel management.

Of all people, Ang Temba Sherpa came in. He is guiding an expedition to Everest base camp, and says there were several groups on their way up. His is a group of 19, and includes men and women from America, India, and Japan.

Karla and I decided to hike up to Khundi and see the Hillary school and hospital, which we did. It was quite a climb, but worth it. We walked across the airfield up there, which seems to us that it might be at too high an altitude to be practical. To fly in there from a much lower elevation would surely be flirting with altitude sickness.

Karla did some good trading today. She traded some clothes that we were going to give away anyway for a small Buddha made of green jade or glass, which I really like, and two carved wooden shells with beetles inside.

Ang Temba says there are 8 or 9 flights coming into Lukla daily, so we should have no problem getting out if the weather is good. Tomorrow is Saturday and we plan to spend some time at the market place before heading down.

March 13.

The market was very busy. Sonam Sherpa and his wife were there buying their weekly supplies. It was fun to walk through the market and see all the various items that were for sale. We left Namche at 9:30 a.m., and arrived in Phakding at 2:20 p.m.. There are lots of expedition boxes heading up. There was a Nepalese and Indian women's expedition that had many large, blue boxes with the name of the expedition printed on their sides. There was an American expedition with more blue boxes, and plastic containers as well. We passed many of each today.

Kanjee is going home for the night. We passed her husband on the trail, he is headed for Namche. We have seen no emotion displayed between sexes.

We were remarking that we had not seen a pregnant woman while in Nepal, but Karla said she saw one and maybe two today.

We are both tired for some reason, even though we are going lower in altitude. There was lots of traffic on the trail. The woman who operates the lodge where we are staying here in Phakding is very nice. She brought us warm water to wash with.

It's 3:30 p.m., and we are the only ones here so far. We are thinking about hot showers and doing laundry in Kathmandu the day after tomorrow. There is a good fire going in the stove, and we are wondering what to have for supper. We are still the only ones here, but the woman says that's OK because we are older people and appreciate the quiet. She's right!

It is now 5:45 p.m., and it has warmed up a bit outside and the wind has stopped.

We have been joined by a German couple who have climbed Island Peak. They said the last 200 meters took four hours because they needed ice screws and because they had no porter and their packs were very heavy.

Many of the Germans who we met smoke, and then complain because they have altitude problems. I think they might be behind the U.S. in smoking awareness. We are having an interesting conversation with them. They trek unfrequented routes. Six years ago they trekked into Dhaulagiri base camp and got snowed in. They ran out of food and only had one package of biscuits to last five days.

Karla with Ama Dablam in the background.

It is now 7:06 p.m., and not long until bedtime. For supper I had daal bhaat again, it was pretty good. Karla had fried potatoes with vegetables and yak cheese.

We are having fun whistling and singing "Jishim Firiri" to a little boy here. It's a very popular tune in Nepal. He thinks it is funny that we can't get the words right. He knows them well, as does about everyone else in Nepal, I think. He drew a picture of his house for us in pencil.

March 14.

We were on the trail at 8:30 a.m.. The little boy we met yesterday evening cried when we left. We were in Lukla at 11:00 a.m.. A leisurely day, we walked around town after getting our sunny corner room at the K2 Lodge, where we took a 45 minute nap at 2:00 p.m..

We counted our money again and paid Kanjee, and we gave her a bag of clothes as a tip. She seemed pleased. We asked her to write her name and address, but she had never gone to school and could not write her name, at least in English letters. So with the help of the hotel people, Karla wrote it down, in care of the K2 Lodge. The lodge owners are taking care of our airplane ticket confirmation.

March 15.

We are scheduled for the first flight out of Lukla. It's a sunny morning here.

It snowed last night above town, but the sun has already melted it off.

At the lodge, the woman put some hot coals and what might have been some cedar in an urn. It smelled like incense, and she swung it about in each room before hanging it outside the window, as did other houses in view. She said it was "for the lama."

Ang Temba was at the airfield. Karla had another photo session, and an airport security man also wanted his photo taken. Due to fog in Kathmandu, flights had been delayed, and our plane was two hours late.

We had a good flight, and we are now in our room at the Nepal View Hotel in Kathmandu. Had a hot shower which felt great, turned in our laundry, and now we are ready for lunch. We might have to move to a common room if one becomes available. It's now 7:30 p.m., and I'm writing this by candle light, as the electricity has been off for a while.

We walked to the super market this afternoon, looking for a small size hair spray, but to no avail. At another shop, I bought an ice screw, a shirt, and a pair of trousers for a total of about $9.00 U.S.. That about does it for my shopping, except I will get a couple more ice screws as a gift to a climber friend back home. I do want to find a Kitaro tape to play when we get back to the states. Tomorrow we will continue our search for some yak cheese to take home too. Also we must confirm our reservations on Thai Airlines for the nineteenth.

We discovered a stupa on our way to the supermarket and there were prayer flags for sale. We also want a yak bell or two, but I will turn the shopping over to Karla now. She bought a few more post cards and stamps. She leads me safely around this city, otherwise I think I would be lost most of the time. We are still waiting for the electricity to come on before going out to supper.

The lights came on at 8:00 p.m., so we are off for a good meal at the Tibetan Kitchen. Karla couldn't eat all of hers so we had it wrapped and gave it to a beggar in the street.

March 16.

After a good night's sleep, we found our way to "Mike's Breakfast" this morning and pigged out on an American style breakfast. We are now back at the hotel, relaxing and writing cards after confirming our flight out on the 19th. We are trying to budget so that we don't have many Rupees left over.

There seems to be more and more foreigners on the streets. We pass the immigration office with a feeling of relief that we don't have to apply for trekking permits now, with the long lines and the time spent waiting.

This afternoon we went to the café and saw Sally's friend. She wants us to take a letter back to Sally. She told us of her trip to Tibet, and about bringing a boy back across the border. Quite a tale. We bought a bundle of 25 prayer flags for Sally.

After eating supper at Helen's, we returned to the hotel and were asked to change to a room with a common bath, which we had agreed to do earlier. It's not bad except there is no place to hang things. It is 7:30 p.m., and our bodies are still on trekking time. We are both tired but will try to read a while before we turn in. We will have to come up with something to do tomorrow.

March 17.

We still have our persistent coughs. Mine loosened up somewhat, but Karla's is still tight. Had breakfast at Mike's again this morning. Great orange juice and food. We caught a 3-wheeler to Baktapur and spent the day there. That area of the city has narrow streets and old buildings with a sort of medieval architecture. The area was dirty, and the people appeared to be very poor. We knew we were getting conned by a school boy, but we let him guide us and we bought a dictionary for him. Karla wrote his name and a short message in it. He is a smart kid, we hope he keeps the book.

We got a close look at a student demonstration in the street near our hotel. Demonstrators carried red flags. There were at least a couple of hundred of them, accompanied by two vans loaded with police. We ducked into a doorway to let them pass. There was a student killed yesterday at the university, by a rival student group. He was cremated today at Pashnituper, a place where many Nepalese are cremated and their ashes scattered in the river.

At the Kathmandu Guest House are banners welcoming the 40th anniversary of the British Everest expedition. We are curious as to whether Hillary will be attending.

This is a "no electricity" evening until 8:30 p.m.. We walked about a bit to see how the shops were managing. Many have white gas lanterns, some have candles, and a few of the larger places have their own small generators. Ate supper at the hotel this evening.

March 18.

Ah, breakfast at Mike's again. The food and atmosphere is well worth the walk. After breakfast we paid the hotel bill, I bought another shirt, and Karla had a minor jean repair done by a tailor. Then back to the room and packed for tomorrow's flight.

We had a relaxing day, reading and mostly taking it easy. We still have nagging coughs, but then most people here seem to have the same. It is now 7:30 p.m., and we are sleepy. We are still on trekking time. We will try to be at the airport between 11:30 tomorrow morning and noon.

March 19.

It is 12:50 p.m., and we are in the Kathmandu airport waiting to board the plane to Bangkok. We had one last breakfast at Mike's this morning, and now we are looking forward to a meal on Thai Airlines this afternoon. We have only Rs. 190 in Nepalese currency, and we will put it in a Red Cross donation box that we noticed in the airport. We have checked our duffles straight through to LAX, as we did not want the hassle of keeping them overnight with us in Bangkok.

After our lengthy but fruitless search for Yak (nak) cheese, the hotel finally made a phone call and we had 1 kilo delivered, so we have it now in Karla's duffle. I hope it doesn't spoil before we get home.

It is now 7:15 p.m., and we are in the Bangkok airport. We have reserved a day room here for 6 hours. Our flight leaves at 7:45 in the morning. Karla has been feeling a bit sick. I'm thinking about getting a haircut while we are waiting.

I just finished reading "A Brief History of Time." Now I am amusing myself by giving scowling looks to people who are lighting up in the no smoking area. Some move elsewhere, some do not. I think most of them have not noticed the no smoking sign.

March 20.

The day room was great. There was free water and sodas in the small fridge. Karla is still having stomach problems and was up during the night. She has some medicine in her duffle, but that is checked. We asked Thai Airline personnel if we could get at her luggage, and they found it in the baggage container and they helped her get her medicine out. Lucky! Thai Airlines also gave us a free breakfast in the transit restaurant.

This is a nice, clean, big airport. We can see our plane, a huge, two story, four engine airliner. Painted on its side is the name "Harphunchai" which we learn was given to it in a Buddhist ceremony.

We must remember all we can of our trip, the good and the bad as well as the beautiful. The cities were interesting, but the beauty, for us, truly belongs to the countryside, the people, and the mountains.

* * * * *

*I know a small grassy flat
where two narrow mountain streams join,
and flakes of black obsidian lay scattered
on the rocky soil
like tiny leaves
after a fall windstorm.*

*Arrowheads, knives,
awls and spear points whisper
of some unknown happening
that left their makers
not enough life or time
to take their treasures with them.*

*I know old stream beds
whose banks are straight and deep
and the dry air has preserved
the protruding horns and skulls
and bones of buffalo
that rest beneath a covering
of soft, brown earth,
which is in turn blanketed
by buffalo grass,
pale green sage, greasewood,
and sometimes meadow larks.*

* * * * *

Aravaipa Canyon

It is the middle of December, and the cool waters of Aravaipa Creek come midway to our knees as we wade our way into this beautiful canyon hidden in the rocky hill country of southeast Arizona. Drawn once more to this place by its beauty and solitude, and the chance for some welcome sun and warmth, this is our second trip here in three years.

Our first trip, also in December, we entered from the west. The weather was wonderful, with daytime temperatures in the high sixties and seventies, a real treat for two Montanans from the wintry western slopes of the northern Rockies. Our days were spent exploring some of the many beautiful side canyons that enter the main one every so often. One of our fondest memories was of going for a swim in a lovely pool carved from the solid rock of a stream bed high up from the main canyon floor, and it was on that trip that we saw our first coati-mundi, a raccoon-like creature that inhabits this area.

Now, however, we are prepared for wet weather. On our way in on Klondyke road there was a dusting of snow in the high country, and we were somewhat apprehensive about what kind of a trip is ahead of us. Rain showers were forecast for the canyon area, but we hoped that in lower elevations there would be little chance for snow.

We walk on, setting ourselves no distance goal, other

than to go deep into the canyon and find a spot for our tent. From there we plan to explore side canyons and just relax for a few days. The air is moist, misty, and smells of vegetation and water. Aravaipa Creek is one of the few streams in southern Arizona that flows year-round, and large sycamore, ash, cottonwood and willow grow along its banks. There are no marked trails, and at times we wonder if we are taking the easy way or the hard way as we continue on.

Sometimes we are able to walk on dry ground for several hundred yards before being forced back into the water, knee deep in places, by the towering canyon walls. As we round a bend, a small band of javalina are quenching their thirst along the stream edge in front of us, and as they become aware of our presence, disappear into the brush and rocks with soft grunts of alarm.

At times the sun breaks through threatening clouds to bathe the canyon walls in gold, turning little ripples in the brown-gray stream into threads of silver. We see some horse tracks along a short stretch of trail, and recall reading that Apache Indians and U.S. Cavalry alike used this passage in the not so distant past.

We pass huge cottonwood trees lying in piles twenty feet and higher off the canyon floor, uprooted and placed there at random by the flash floods that the area is subject to. We try to imagine what it must be like here during one of these holocausts, flood waters roaring and foaming through the canyon, carrying debris and boulders along as it thunders its way downstream. We remain aware of the possibility of a flood happening, and camp with an escape route readily available.

Campsites in the canyon are primitive, and one can camp where one likes. We search for a place on the north side, in a relatively wide area that will allow a maximum of sunlight. At last we come upon a suitable site, at the mouth of a small but steep side canyon, complete with hidden waterfall and an inviting game trail. In no time the tent is up and a small fire going, fueled by bark from a downed cottonwood next to our camp. Ordinarily we would rely on our backpacking stove alone, but tonight there is a chill in the air, and a fire feels good. Clouds have disappeared, and stars dot the night sky while beams of moonlight start to find their way down the canyon walls. The evening meal finished, we lay in our tent in the darkness, listening to the soft hoot-hoot of an owl perched in a tree across the canyon floor.

The next two days are spent exploring side canyons and relaxing in camp. At times we are forced to make our own trail through the sharp rock and thick groves of brush and cacti as we climb upward through ever narrowing crevices. On one of our hikes along the creek, we spot a band of desert bighorn sheep high above a sheer rock wall, grazing on desert grasses along the edge of the gorge. An occasional hawk circles above, keen eyes scanning the canyon below for prey.

Each bend presents new vistas, huge trees, green grassy slopes, towering walls reaching upwards toward the heavens. Always there is the gentle murmur of the stream as it slowly carves the canyon ever deeper.

Daytime temperatures manage to get no higher than in the fifties, and in the morning there is a skim of thin ice along the waters edge. The hillside from behind camp to the base of the cliffs is dotted with a variety of cactus, ranging from prickly pear and ocotillo to giant saguaro which provide homes for a few of the more than 200 species of birds that have been seen here. Some birds more commonly found in Mexico often visit this haven. There is the ever present sign of javalina, tracks left by their sharply pointed hooves, rocky soil turned over in their rooting search for food. Tracks of deer and coati-mundi are common in the sandy soil along the stream.

Our last night in camp we treat ourselves by roasting pinion nuts that we brought in, savoring each one and making ecstatic comments when we bite into one that is roasted to a particularly fine flavor. This evening we are treated to a colorful sunset, viewed through a window formed by the towering canyon walls, clouds tinted with shades of red and purple and gold.

Ghosts of ancient peoples are here in this lonely place. You can feel their presence, smell the smoke of their campfires. How long ago? No one knows for sure. Potsherds and other artifacts show that people have inhabited the area for centuries.

On the morning we must leave, the sky is gray and threatening, and we expect rain. We are hesitant at first to step into the creek, but do so with bravado; our heavy wool socks become instantly soaked, yet they keep our feet reasonably warm. On our hike out, we realize how fortunate we are to have been able to experience this wilderness, this place where we could come and be renewed. We leave the canyon as we found it, only our footprints remain to show that we were here, and they will soon be washed away by the winter rains.

No machines intrude here, no trail bikes, no ORV's. Only hikers and horseback riders are allowed to enter. This canyon was first declared a primitive area in 1969, and in 1984 Congress designated it as a wilderness area. It is now managed by the Bureau of Land Management, and is a monument to those far sighted individuals who understand the human need for places such as Aravaipa Canyon.

* * * * *

*I know a quiet place
that water carved,
where the rushing, boiling
current is cleaved
by granite rock.*

*The pool below this rock
is deep and calm,
a place where no white water
enters even in the spring
when rains and melting snow
roar thundering down the canyon.*

* * * * *

Olympic Peninsula

March 22, 1989

Karla and I drove up the Olympic Peninsula coast in Washington to La Push and then to Rialto Beach. We spent the night at a National Park campground, and decided to hike north on the beach.

March 23.

We backpacked north to the site of the Chilean Monument to the wreck of a schooner that happened in 1920. On the way we found a dead sea lion on the beach. Slow going, lots of rocks, we hiked 2 ½ miles in 3 ½ hours. It is a stormy day, but not too bad. There is a strong wind and some sunshine. The surf is high.

After making camp we watched the tide come in and enjoyed a supper of Spanish rice, fresh asparagus, and tea. While viewing the surf we saw two bald eagles being chased by gulls. It is now 6:30 p.m., and we are ready for bed. The surf is noisy, we may need earplugs.

On the beach below our camp on the Olympic Peninsula.

March 24.

We awoke to a hard rain. We had oatmeal and tea, and then spent a couple of hours beach combing in the rain. It kept raining until noon and we got a bit wet. We saw lots of gulls and a bald eagle feeding on some kind of snails attached to a coil of rope and a piece of net. We went back to our tent for some hot tea, and after a while the rain stopped.

It is 5:00 p.m., and it has been raining off and on all afternoon. We stayed in the tent. Karla has been reading "The Snow Leopard." I have read info on the Olympic coast. We have both checked and re-checked the tide tables. There are two backpackers walking on the beach, heading north. They will have to hurry to make it around the headlands before the incoming tide makes the route impassable

Earlier, at 4:00 p.m., we ate our big daily meal of macaroni with spaghetti sauce. I spilled some of the macaroni when the lid fell off the pot while draining it. We drank the bottle of Rainier Ale that I had packed in. We washed dishes and filled the pots with water for breakfast. We have been getting water from a small creek below camp and treating it with iodine tablets. Again we watch the tide come in. According to the tide tables, the high tide should be 6 feet at 6:18 p.m..

The sun broke through the clouds briefly for a beautiful but cloudy sunset. We took a couple of photos, washed the supper dishes, and were in our sleeping bags at 7:00 p.m., to read for awhile before sleeping.

March 25.

It was raining lightly as we ate breakfast at 7:00 a.m., but it stopped long enough for us to get our tent down and packed. We got started on our way back at 8:40 a.m., and it began raining again. It continued to be wet and windy all the way back. We were finally soaked, but not really cold. The hike back to our vehicle took 3 hours. On the way we saw a raccoon, limpets, snails, crabs, dead starfish, gulls. We don't know why none of the birds or animals are eating the dead sea lion.

When we get back to "Old Blue," our pickup, we fill the front seat area with wet things and turn the heater on high. We head up the road to Forks to replenish our groceries, then on to the Ozette ranger station where we will spend the night sleeping in the camper shell on the pickup, then backpack to the coast again. It's a nine mile triangular trip to Cape Alava, Sand Point, then back to the ranger station. We will spend tomorrow night camped in our tent on the coast.

A pesky raccoon tried to beg food from us while we were eating supper tonight. The weather forecast is for more wet and windy weather tomorrow.

March 26.

It was raining lightly when we awoke. We followed a cedar boardwalk through moss, ferns and huge trees for 3.3 miles to the coast. We saw lots of deer at Cape Alava. We must have passed the petroglyphs without knowing, we didn't see them anyway. We saw lots of interesting stuff on the beach though, including a dead seal pup, bald eagles, deer and one golden eagle. There are lots of rocks off shore.

We planned on camping about 2 miles down the coast, but we found ourselves at Sand Point, a distance of 3 miles, before we realized it. We found a camp site and put the tent up, but could tell that we had more wind than we wanted so we moved our tent to a sheltered site. We have a good view of the shore just a few yards below our tent. It didn't rain much at all today. We watched a fine sunset and went to bed at 7:00 p.m.. The moon and stars are out tonight. Out on the horizon we can see ships headed north.

March 27.

We were up at 6:30 a.m., and had breakfast on the beach by our tent site. No rain. We watched gulls feeding while we ate. We packed up, hiked back to the ranger station and drove to Port Angeles for a sea food fix. Port Angeles seems like a nice place to live, we decide.

We had good views of the Olympic Range today. It's 4:15 p.m., and I am writing this while waiting at Kingston for the next ferry to Edmonds. We got here just as one was pulling out. The Cascades are visible and appear to have a dusting of fresh snow on them. We are heading for home, and will go by way of Snowqualmie Pass to Ellensburg, then on to Moses Lake where we plan to spend the night. Then back to our house in Montana. We had a memorable time hiking and camping on the Pacific coast. It was good to be hiking along the ocean again.

Vancouver Island, B.C.

Inland Passage sea kayak trip

September 7, 2001.

After making the necessary arrangements for our kayak trip, we moved our camp to Sea View Campground at Telegraph Cove, near Johnstone Strait. Afterward, we had time to do our laundry and take a walk around the dock area.

When we returned to our camp, we packed dry bags for our kayak trip tomorrow, and went to bed early.

September 8.

This morning at 9:00 a.m., we were at the North Island kayak office near the marina. There we met our guide and the rest of our group, which will include two women from Germany who will share a double kayak, and a man and woman from England who will also share a double kayak. Karla and I share a double also. Our guide has a single.

It was a cold, drizzly morning as we loaded our kayaks and finally left the dock at 10:30 a.m.. Adam, our guide, said that we would not stop for lunch, but would paddle straight to our first camp site. As we paddled we saw a group of Orcas that were very close to us. There were also hundreds of jumping salmon all around us. With the wind and tide at our backs, we arrived there at 2:30 p.m.. There was still quite a bit of wind, but the sun was shining.

Karla and I set up our tent in a spot overlooking the strait. We built a campfire and had a meal of veggie burritos and fresh baked brownies.

September 9.

Everyone was up and ready for breakfast by 8:00 a.m.. We had granola with fruit and yogurt. The wind was still blowing, but the sun was shining. We got into our kayaks and paddled downwind for an hour or so, to a nice beach. As we paddled we saw Dall's Porpoises, more Orcas, and more jumping salmon.

A purse seiner had set up in a cove near the beach, and Adam paddled out to get a salmon from them for our evening meal.

After a cold lunch of bagels and cheese, we had a hard paddle back to our campsite. Karla tried the rear position in our kayak, which involves using the foot pedals that operate the steering rudder.

We had a great meal of seafood chowder, the fresh salmon, smoked oysters, muscles, clams and sourdough bread along with Danish rolls for dessert. Afterwards, we hiked behind camp in the early evening, and later had another nice campfire on the beach.

September 10.

Today is Karla's birthday. Breakfast at 8:00 a.m. consisted of oatmeal, granola and fruit. After breakfast we took down our tents and loaded our gear into our kayaks. We paddled for a couple of hours to a small, hidden cove where we set up camp. At this site there are sunny rocks to bask on and look out at Georgia Strait. It is a beautiful, calm and sunny day. The water is flat and smooth.

We have learned that one has to be familiar with tides to navigate these waters in sea kayaks. Some of the narrow routes between the islands have to be traveled at slack tide, otherwise the tides cause very swift currents to flow that would be very dangerous for anyone in a kayak.

Today we saw some river otter, harbor porpoises, Stellar sea lions (very close), bald eagles, blue herons and more jumping salmon. In the secluded little cove where we camped we paddled over an octopus that was very near shore.

After a meal of stir-fried vegetables and noodles, we sat around our campfire and talked. We sang "Happy Birthday" to Karla. The small group of people that we are paddling with are very nice and enjoyable to be with.

September 11.

Pancakes and fruit for breakfast at 8:00 a.m., and after taking our tents down and packing our gear we were on the water at 10:15. The weather was nice. On the way back across the strait to Telegraph Cove, we were paddling against the incoming tide, so even though there was no wind and the water was flat, it was still a hard crossing.

When we arrived back at our starting point, a guide came down to help us unload our gear. He immediately informed us of the planes crashing into the World Trade Center in New York City. We did not believe him, and accused him of making it up.

I went to our vehicle and turned on the radio, and sure enough there were reports of the tragic events in New York. Everyone remembers where they were when those sort of things happen, and we will always remember that we were just getting out of our sea kayaks after a camping trip just off Vancouver Island on the Inland Passage when we learned of the terrorist attack.

Gary Yates

* * * * *

Northern Lights

By chance I woke,
and saw through sleep filled eyes
scenes framed in dark shadow
of fragrant fir and pine,
faintly glowing embers in campfire ash,
countless rubies set in faded gray.

Wondering, my vision climbed
from grassy carpet to granite crags
draped with snowy lace whose moonlit strands
lay sparkling 'neath the star filled universe
where crescent moon, now almost full,
cast pale glow to all below.

And then some distant curtain rose
and bid the overture begin.

Horizons burned with ice blue flame
while wave after jagged wave of paler shades
ascended on soundless wings
the indigo depths of endless space.

Summits and Trails

*Flashing liquid silver, left where once were stars
shimmering, ragged, rippling pools of turquoise light,
jewels on velvet night.*

*Unseen trumpets gave clarion call
from mighty halls in that great inverted bowl
and violins, cellos, flutes played
dreamlike sounds that deceived the ears.*

*From hiding places by rocks and trees
blue shadows flew to dance and sway
with this incredible display
and when it seemed the crystal stage
could hold no more,
choral voices joined the strings
and a thousand colors played notes
never heard before.*

*Then the hills themselves arose
from their earthly bed
with fir and pine and rock strewn slopes
to greet the laser beams of jade and gold
that hurtled from pole to distant pole.*

*To this magical score there seemed no end,
but then, the heavens let the painting fade,
and softly, gently, the curtain fell,
and moon and stars returned once more.*

* * * * *

Printed in the United States
40549LVS00002B/247-252